The Patter

A guide to current Glasgow usage

Michael Munro

Drawings by David Neilson

Glasgow District Libraries
1985

© Michael Munro 1985.

Drawings © David Neilson 1985.

ISBN 0-906169-09-7.

Published by Glasgow District Libraries Publications Board, The Mitchell Library, North Street, Glasgow G3 7DN.

Typeset and printed by Holmes McDougall Ltd., 24 Clydeholm Road, Clydeside Industrial Estate, Glasgow G14 0AU.

INTRODUCTION

This little book was conceived as a defining guide to the language of the big bad beautiful city of Glasgow. The language is that to be heard in the city's homes and public places, often on television and radio, and sometimes read in newspapers, magazines, or books: the contemporary urban Scots dialect of Glasgow.

As the subtitle makes clear the primary criterion for including items of vocabulary is that they must be current or, in a few cases, on the verge of disappearing from common use. This is not because I believe the dialect of today to be in any way superior or more worthy of recording than that of the past. It is probably too late to document the Glasgow parlance of previous generations — mainly because it rarely found its way into print — and much of interest will have been lost without trace. There is little to be gained from lamenting this loss. Every living language is subject to an inevitable and continuous process of change and only a romantic would dream of halting this evolution. Consigning archaic Glaswegian to the social historian or linguistic researcher I made it my aim to survey just one period of Glasgow usage, that of today.

With the mass media firmly in control of contemporary thought and communication, regional dialects are now more than ever at risk of dilution or total disappearance, and local slang, like any slang, is by its nature ephemeral. I would hope that by recording it in this book some of this particular dialect will at least be 'fixed' in print before it too is forgotten in everyday use.

While concentrating on words exclusive to Glasgow I thought it helpful to include a proportion of Scots material having a wider geographical spread. Sometimes this was because a word has a specific Glasgow twist to its general meaning but more often because the word is part of the everyday speech of Glasgow and as much of a puzzle to speakers of 'Standard English' as the bona fide Glaswegianisms.

The speech of the Glaswegian has been much maligned. Even natives of the city have joined in yoking it with illiteracy and stigmatizing it as ignorant corruption of the Queen's English. No help has been given by various jokey books about Glasgow parlance that contrive to present it as a language for inarticulate idiots. I will admit that Glaswegian at its broadest has idiosyncratic habits that the purist condemns as slovenly but I would immediately add that these are no more *intrinsically* deplorable or deserving of contempt than the slurs, elisions, and lazy pronunciation common to that dialect which, through prevalence at the English Court and enshrinement by the B.B.C., has come to be regarded as 'good' English.

3

I maintain that Glaswegian is a rich, vital, and above all valid regional dialect which gives a true reflection of the city and its inhabitants with all their unattractive features, such as deprivation, bigotry, and pugnacity, but with all their virtues too, such as robust and irreverent humour, resilience, and abhorrence of pretension.

A note on the treatment of material

This is not intended to be a scholarly work of lexicography. While having the serious intention of recording the language I could see no reason to scorn entertaining the native as well as enlightening the foreigner and have therefore tried to maintain a lighthearted tone in the definitions and illustrative examples.

I have not dealt with etymology to any great extent except where I consider it verifiable (often difficult with any dialect or slang) and entertaining or interesting to the reader. On the subject of orthography, it should be borne in mind that a good many of these terms may never have been written down before, let alone printed. Accordingly, in my spelling of words included I have considered myself free to use versions that seem sensible to me, trying to come close to how the words are pronounced (without aiming at a completely phonetic transliteration) but sometimes bowing to useful long-established versions. For example, I have preferred *aw* to *a'* and have tried consistently to do without apostrophes except in a case like *gie's* (which I prefer to *geez*) where the apostrophe shows that the pronunciation still has two components in most contexts.

I have regarded the *-y* and *-ie* endings as equivalent in most cases, using the form that seemed right to me, and as for the famous glottal stop (*bo'l* bottle, *men'al* mental, etc.), I have left this to be assumed rather than bombard the reader with a tedious and incomprehensible barrage of apostrophes.

Readers looking for an explanation of an individual word should consult the body of the text where words are defined in alphabetical order. Rhyming slang and common phrases or sayings not easily linked to one key word are dealt with in separate appendices.

Pronunciation

As I am not trying to teach anyone how to speak Glaswegian it was never my intention to give a pronunciation for every word defined. These have only been inserted where they will avoid confusion or help pinpoint something a reader may have heard but fail to recognise when transliterated. However, a few general remarks about Glasgow diction may serve as a rough guide.

It is important for outsiders to realise that all natives of the city do not speak in broad Glaswegian. Variations can always be heard depending on where the speaker comes from, his/her education, and where on the social scale he/she is (or would like you to think he/she is) and Glaswegianisms find their way into the speech of all but the most rarefied strata.

In broad Glaswegian, English words with sounds as in hair, bear, rare, will come out as *herr, berr, rerr*. This process is also shown in Glaswegian pronunciation of Scots words like mair or flair which become *merr* and *flerr*. Similarly, shop, bottle, on, stop, become *shoap, boatle, oan, stoap,* and the Scots stot becomes *stoat*.

Certain words change in pronunciation according to whether or not they are accented e.g.

What like was it? *but* Wan lik that
Whit kind dae ye want? *but* That kinna thing
That's no the right type *but* What tippa motor's that?

An interesting phenomenon in Glaswegian pronunciation is that in many place names consisting of two or more parts Glaswegians tend to emphasise the last part e.g. Nits*hill*, Clyde*bank*, Govan*hill*, Peni*lee*, Gilmore*hill*. This is carried over into the pronunciation of street names eg Stock*well* Street, Ren*field* Street, Sauchie*hall* Street. The native Glaswegian may take his holidays in *Corn*wall and still refer to Corn*wall* Street.

Acknowledgements

My thanks go to: my wife for encouragement and putting up with this small obsession; David Neilson for all his advice and help, not least for his cartoons; Paul Gunnion for reading the typescript; Joe Fisher and Hamish Whyte of The Mitchell Library; all the friends, colleagues, and fellow citizens who, whether they were aware of it or not, suggested material for this book.

A

I know you did it so don't act it with me

a A local form of 'of': 'Two boatles a ginger.'

ablow Below: 'Yer good shoes are in ablow the bed.'

act it To behave in a deliberately obtuse or disingenuous manner; try it on: 'I know you did it so don't act it with me.'

after Indicates that the speaker has just done or had something: 'I'm just after my tea.' 'Ah'm just after bein tae the doctor's'. But if in a pub someone asks you 'What are you after?' this is not an enquiry after your recent doings but an offer to get you a drink.

ages The same age as: 'Your Doreen's ages wi me.'

ahead To **go right ahead** with someone is to come to blows with him: 'Big Shuggy an him was gauny go right ahead.'

aipple A local version of apple.

air The phrase **up in the air** means ruined or ruled out: 'If we canny get booked up for the Fair Fortnight that'll be the hoalidays up in the air.'

airieplane A local version of aeroplane, often shortened to **airie**: 'Ur we gaun up in a big airie Da?'

am ur   Who knows the origins of this bizarre form of I am? Usually used in contradiction, whether positive: 'You're no goin', 'Am ur sot' or negative: 'Am urny goin', 'Aye ye ur', 'No am urny.'

Arab   In Glasgow this has been a term of abuse since even before the rise of the oil sheikhs: 'Get lost ya Arab ye!'

ask   To **ask for** someone is to enquire after his health or send him your regards: 'Tell your mother I was asking for her.' 'Aunty Mary was asking for ye.'

at   A truncated form of that: 'See at man ower there?' If when passing by an informal football game the ball strays in your direction you may hear urgent cries of 'at baw!' (loosely, 'please may we have our ball back?').

at it   Trying it on, up to no good: 'Watch him, he's at it.'

aw   Local form of all: 'At's aw ye're gettin.' 'Ah'm comin an aw.'

away   A multipurpose word. It can express incredulity, whether real or sarcastic: 'Away! Is that right?' 'Away ye go!'
   I'll away, I'll be away, *or* **I'm away** mean 'I'm leaving now.' **Away wi it** means drunk or stupid: 'Leave him alane, he's away wi it.'

awfy   Awful, as in very: 'It wizny awfy good.' 'You're awfy cheeky gettin.'

ayeways   Always.

B

A bear

back   The period just after the hour, as used when arranging a rendezvous: 'I'll see you at the back of five.' This is an elastic period ranging between, say, five past and twenty past the hour.

backie   To **give someone a backie** means either **1.** to help someone climb a wall by offering your bent back as a platform, or **2.** to let someone sit behind you on your bicycle.

backs   The area at the rear of a tenement building, divided into **back courts** or **back greens**, one to each close.

bachle *or* **bauchle**   A small, usually old or misshapen person; often used as an insult: 'Away ye go ya wee bachle.'

Bad Fire, the   Hell: 'If ye don't eat yer carrots ye'll go to the Bad Fire.'

bag   To **give someone the bag** is to sack him.

baggies *or* **baggie-minnies**   Minnows or, sometimes, sticklebacks, as hunted by children with nets and jamjars.

bahookie   A nicely cheeky word for backside: 'Shift yer big bahookie till I get a seat.'

8

baldy A very short haircut: 'That was a right baldy ye got.'

Baldy Bayne A nickname applied to any bald man. I don't know if an original existed but there is at least one pub that bears the name.

baldy crust Another name for any bald man, but also applied to the bald pate itself: 'You'll know him by his old baldy crust.'

balloon An empty boaster, a blowhard: 'Don't listen to that big balloon.'

bammy Local version of barmy, i.e. insane: 'That bammy brother a hers has smashed his motor again.'

bampot *or* **bamstick** An idiot, fool, or sometimes a nutcase. This is often shortened to **bam**, and any eccentric named Thomas risks being dubbed 'Tam the Bam.'

bandit A general term of abuse. The kind of thing a more polite person might exclaim on hitting his thumb with a hammer: 'Ahya bandit!' Probably a euphemism.

banjo (pronounced ban-*jo*) to hit someone a single very hard blow: 'John just banjoed the wan nearest him an got aff his mark.'

banker In betting circles, a sure thing: 'Never mind giein us any mair a yer bankers.'

baries The bare feet: 'I hate walkin on lino in my baries.'

Bar-L Nickname for Barlinnie Prison, and also for the Barlanark area of the city.

barra Barrow. When someone says 'That's right inty ma barra' this means 'That suits me fine.' To 'fancy your barra' means to have a high opinion of yourself. **Wee barra** is a genial term of address for a small person: 'Gaun yersel wee barra!'

Barras, the Of course, Glasgow's renowned informal shopping complex, east of Glasgow Cross. Its proverbial place in the language is shown by such phrases as 'I bet she didn't get *that* at the Barras' meaning 'That was certainly not cheap.'

bat A blow, especially as in 'a bat in the mouth.'

batter To be **on the batter** is to be on a drinking spree. Perhaps this derives from the worse-for-wear condition of those indulging in this pastime.

bawface   A big round face or someone having one.

bawheid   Roughly the same as bawface but also common as a disrespectful form of address: 'Hey bawheid! C'mere till Ah laugh at ye!'

beamer   A bright red blush: 'Ye should've seen her face — what a beamer!'

bear   A name loosely applied to any noisy or belligerent young man, usually a heavy drinker, varying from the merely boisterous to the positively dangerous. A pub frequented by many of these is known as a **bearpit**: 'Ah wiz oot wi ma wee cousin an his mates; a right crowd a bears they were an aw.'

beardie   A nickname for any man with a beard. Also, when a man tickles a child by rubbing his stubbly cheek on the child's face he is said to give the child **a beardie**.

beast   To **get beasted in** is to eat heartily and without standing on ceremony: 'There's yer tea oot boys — get beasted in.'

beauty   **Ya beauty** is a common exclamation of delight: 'Nae school fur seven weeks! Ya beauty!'

bed-recess   In a tenement flat, an alcove or recess in, for example, the kitchen which formerly held a boxed-in or curtained-off bed. These are now often used as dining areas.

beds   Hopscotch, also known as **peever**. The word beds strictly applies to the actual layout for the game as chalked on a pavement.

bee-heided   Scatter-brained, forgetful, distracted: 'Ma man's that bee-heided he canny mind his ain phone number.'

beelin   Absolutely furious: 'Mind the aul man dizny get ye — he's beelin the night.' Also used to describe a spot, boil, etc., that is full of pus.

beezer   An extremely cold, icy day: 'I'm no goin oot the day, it's a beezer alright.'

bell   If it's your round in the pub you are said to be **on the bell**: 'Just you sit on yer backside, I'm on the bell.'

belong   To come from, live in: 'Is there emdy here belongs tae Carntyne?'

belter   Something excellent; anything from a member of the opposite sex to a sunny day.

ben   In, inside, into: 'We'll have our tea ben the room.'

bent shot   A slang term for a homosexual.

berries   To say that something is **the berries** means it's really good, the greatest.

bevvy   **The bevvy** is the drink, alcohol, booze. **A bevvy** is a drink or a drinking session. To be **on the bevvy** is to be drinking; **on the heavy bevvy** is drinking to excess. **To bevvy** is to drink (alcohol). To be **bevvied** is to be drunk. A **bevvy-merchant** is not a vendor of alcohol but a drunkard.

Bhoys, the   Nickname for Celtic F.C.

biddy *or* **red biddy**   Cheap strong red wine, as consumed by down-and-outs.

Billy *or* **Billy-boy**   A Protestant (derives from William of Orange): 'Are you a Billy or a Tim?'

binger   In betting circles, a losing bet: 'Ah've had nothing but bingers aw day.'

black-affronted   Ashamed, mortified, or offended: 'I was black-affronted when I went to pay and couldn't find my purse.'

bladder   A leather football as opposed to a plastic one: 'Away an see if yer big brother'll gie us a len a his bladder.'

blinder   Either a drinking spree: 'He went on a blinder', or an excellent game or performance: 'The goalie played a blinder.'

bloodsucker   A typically ghoulish children's name for a large earthworm.

blooter   To kick something (usually a football) fiercely and often wildly: 'The big defender just blootered it up the park.' **Blootered** is a slang word for drunk.

blue   Rangers F.C. are sometimes referred to as **the boys in (royal) blue** or the **Light Blues**.

bluenose   Nickname for a Rangers supporter: 'Her aul boy's a right bluenose.'

Blythswood Square   Proverbial city-centre haunt of prostitutes.

body   A bored football fan, perhaps having abandoned hope of seeing a goal and prepared to settle for a bit of mayhem instead, may exhort his heroes to greater commitment by crying: 'C'moan gie's a boady!'

body swerve   Avoiding action, a dodge. This is one of a number of football terms that have passed into everyday parlance: 'I'm meant to be goin to my old dear's but I think I'll give it a body swerve.' This is sometimes shortened to **swerve**: 'I never saw ye at the meetin.' 'Naw, Ah swerved it an went hame.'

bogey[1]   A child's cart made from miscellaneous bits of wood or boxes and the wheels from an old pram.

bogey[2]   When something, not necessarily a game, arrives at a stalemate or deadlock people often say 'The game's a bogey.'

boggin   Smelly, stinking: 'Sumdy's feet are boggin.'

boke *or* **boak**   To **boke** is to vomit or make someone sick: 'He's boked aw doon his jaiket.' 'Would that no boke ye?' To **give someone the boke** is to nauseate or make him sick, and as dry retching is more horrible than vomiting so **the dry boke** is the apotheosis of disgust: 'See you, ye gie me the dry boke.'
    Boky means nauseous: 'Feelin boky son?' **Boky-fu** means drunk or over-stuffed with food to the point of feeling sick.

bombed out   Rejected, out of the question: 'That's that idea bombed out then.' 'Ye're bombed out, squire.'

books   To **get your books** means to get the sack.

boot   To **stick the boot on** someone is to kick him: 'Never mind the kung-fu: stick the boot on the big animal!'

Boots' Corner   The sheltered entranceway to Boots department store on the corner of Argyle Street and Union Street is a famous trysting place. To be left alone and palely loitering here is the height of humiliation.

bothy   Originally applied to a labourers' shelter on a building site, this term is still used for the more sophisticated portakabins. I have even heard it used for the workers' cloakroom in a factory.

bowf *or* **bouf**   To **bowf** is to stink: 'That bin's bowfin.' **A bowf** is an offensive smell and a **honkin bowf** is an extreme example.

bowly   Bandy-legged.

box   A slang word for brain or head; especially in **out yer box** which means insensibly drunk. Something that is very difficult to understand may be said to **do your box in**: 'See that algebra? Ah'm nae use at it — it jist does ma box in.'

brain   **Out yer brain** and **brainless** are both terms for drunk and incapable.

brammer   Anything excellent: 'Your new suit's a brammer.'

breenge   **To breenge** is to rush impetuously forward, leap without looking: 'He just breenged oot the door an took a heider doon the stairs.' **A breenge** is a mad heedless dash: 'The visitors' tactics in the second half degenerated to a combination of the long clearance and the big breenge up the park.' A **breenger** is a rash impetuous person, someone who rushes into things.

bricks   If someone is long-established in a place or organisation or has been involved since the beginning he may be described as being **in with the bricks**.

brig   The old Scots word for bridge survives in the local pronunciation of certain Glasgow place-names, eg Brigton (Bridgeton) and The Briggait (Bridgegate).

broo   A shorter form of **burroo**.

bubble   To weep: 'What are you bubblin for?' Also an instance of this: 'I had a wee bubble.' Someone who is in tears or sulking may be called **bubbly**: 'Are you comin or no? Ach well stick, bubbly!'

bucket   A substantial amount to drink: 'I had a right bucket last night.' To **take a good bucket** means to be a heavy drinker.

buckie-up   This means the same as **backie** in the sense of climbing: 'Sumdy gie's a buckie-up.'

bug   To **let bug** is to let on, tell others what you are planning: 'You an me'll slip out for a jar — don't let bug to the rest.'

bug-ladders   Disparaging term for sidewhiskers.

Bully Wee, the   Nickname for Clyde F.C.

bum This is a suitably contemptuous term for a boaster or the kind of egotist who continually spouts about himself. To behave in this way is **to bum**. To **bum your chaff** *or* **load** is to attempt to foist someone off with dubious stories, either to impress or pull the wool over someone's eyes. To **bum something up** is to sing its praises: 'This is no all it's bummed up to be.' 'He's always bummin himsel up.'

bumfle A wrinkle or crease in material. **To bumfle** something or get it **bumfled up** is to wrinkle or crease it.

bummer **Heid bummer** is an irreverent term for a boss or leader: 'Who's the heid bummer around here?'

bun An ugly or disreputable woman: 'Yer mammy's a bun!'

bung A tip, a gratuity. **To bung** someone is to tip him: 'The moolly aul get never gied us a bung.'

bunnit The Glaswegian pronunciation of bonnet (the old-fashioned man's flat cap) but the term is often applied to any man's hat.

burroo *or* **broo** The Department of Health and Social Security. Someone who is out of work and receiving unemployment benefit (**burroo money**) is said to be **on the burroo**. The term originated as a Glasgow pronunciation of bureau as in Employment Bureau, a former name for this institution.

burst To beat up, thrash: 'If I get him I'll burst him.'

but [1] Often tacked on at the end of a sentence containing contradiction: 'He says ye've to go', 'I'm no goin but.' It can also mean 'however' or 'nevertheless': 'Their meat's awfy dear', 'It's good but.'

but [2] A past tense of bite: 'That daft budgie's but ma finger.'

buzz To sniff glue: 'He just started buzzin because there's nuthin else to do round here.'

by Past or over: 'Well, that's the holidays by for another year.' Away, in its place: 'Be a good boy and put your toys by.'
   In by means inside or indoors: 'Ach well, I'll away in by.'

bye Another term from football. In a tournament with an odd number of teams one team may be chosen to advance to the next round without playing a qualifying game. This is called being given a bye. In everyday conversation to **give something a bye** means to avoid it, leave it out, or stop it: 'Goin for a pint?' 'Naw, I'll gie it a bye.' 'Hey you! Gie that carry-on a bye wull ye?'

The Co

cady   Another name for a man's hat.

cakey, caikie   Daft.

canny   A local version of can't: 'Ah canny take it!'

carry-out   Drinks or food bought for consumption elsewhere, take-away: 'We better get a carry-out for this party.' 'We had a chinky carry-out for our tea.'

caur   A motor car: 'The dug got knocked doon wi a caur.'

causey *or* **causeystane**   A cobblestone. A few cobbled streets still exist in older parts of the city: 'He was stuffin his face wi a piece like a causeystane.'

caw *or* **ca**   To **caw the legs from** someone is to sweep his legs from under him; much used in football contexts.

Celts, the   Nickname for Celtic F.C.

chanty-wrastler   A picturesque if vague insulting name. A chanty is a chamberpot and wrastler is a Scots form of wrestler. Could the term denote a menial who empties chamberpots?

15

chap To knock: 'Chap the door an see if they're in.' In dominoes someone who can't play any of his pieces will say he is **chapping**. If someone says 'a chap came to the door' the chances are that what is meant is not 'some fellow called' but 'there was a knock at the door.'

character To **give someone his character** is to give him a piece of your mind, tell him exactly what you think of him, always unflattering.

check To look at, 'get a load of': 'Check that haircut.' 'Check the new jaikit.'

chib A knife or razor used as a weapon. **To chib** someone is to stab or slash him.

chin To accost someone in order to complain or speak to him: 'I just went up and chinned the head waiter.'

chitterin bite A sandwich or snack, especially for eating after swimming, presumably to stop your teeth chittering with cold.

chookie A fool. Also short for **chookiebirdie**, a childish name for a bird. Also used in the contradictory retort **will ye chookie!** meaning 'you certainly will not,' in this case a polite substitution for something stronger.

chow Glasgow version of chew: 'Are you talkin to me or chowin a brick?'

chuckie *or* **chuckiestane** A pebble or small stone: 'Who's flingin chuckies at the windy?'

chute A children's slide: 'Can I get a shot on the chute, mammy?'

Citz, the Nickname for the Citizens' Theatre.

claim To **claim** someone is to tell him that you are out to get him, tell him he is a marked man; often used in the form 'You're claimed.'

clap To **clap** something, especially an animal, is to stroke or pat it. Also a noun: 'Give the nice doggie a wee clap.'

clapped-in Sunken, said of the face or jaws: 'I doubt he's no well; his face is awful clapped-in lookin.' 'The taste a that would clap yer jaws in.'

clappy-doo A kind of large black-shelled mussel, as sold in certain fish shops. The name seems to be a corruption from Gaelic (*dubh* meaning black).

clatty *or* **clarty** Dirty or muddy: 'My shoes are clatty.' 'Away an wash yer hauns ya clatty article.' To call somebody a **clat** means that you think he is dirty, whether physically or mentally.

16

claw   To scratch: 'Stop clawin yer heid; folk'll think ye're lousy.'

Clenny, the   The Corporation Cleansing Department: 'I hear you got a job with the Clenny.' A bin-lorry is sometimes referred to as a **Clenny-motor**.

click   Someone who has succeeded in 'getting off with' a member of the opposite sex may be said to have got a **click**: 'The disco was rubbish. The only one that got a click was wee Susan.'

close   This word applies to the common entrance and hallway of a tenement building and by extension takes in all the flats and occupants of the building as a unit: 'Everybody in the close is getting new windows.' 'Stop shouting — the whole close'll hear you.' The word "up" is usually used in connection with entering or living in a close: 'He's went up the wrang close.' 'She stays up our close.'
   The street entrance to a close is called the **close-mouth** and the rear part of a close is the **back-close**: 'Ye can leave yer bike in the back-close.'

cloy up   To stop talking, shut up.

cludgie *or* **cludge**   A toilet.

clug   To kick, especially an opposing player in a football match. Also used in the form **put the clug on him**, sometimes shouted as advice from the terracing to a player having difficulty in dealing with an elusive dribbler.

clype   **To clype** is to tell tales, to inform on someone, especially at school. A **clype** is someone who does this: 'We're no playin wi you ya wee clype!'

Co, the   Nickname for the Cooperative Society or one of its shops. When given its full title the pronunciation often comes out as coop*era*itive.

coal-carry   A piggyback, obviously likened to being carried as a coalman carries a sack of coal.

come ahead   An exhortation to get a grip on yourself, stop messing about, or sometimes to begin a fight.

come away   Used in shouts of encouragement: 'Come away Scotland!'

coorie in   To cuddle or snuggle up to someone.

cop   To **cop your whack** means to get your share, get what is coming to you, or to get an eyeful of something: 'Cop yer whack for a tin a beer lads.' 'Cop yer whack for they troosers.'

17

corrie-fisted   Left-handed.

coup *or* **cowp**   To spill, overturn, or dump: 'I've couped a pint over my good denims.' 'The big eejit couped the table ower.' 'You're no meant tae coup yer rubbish here.' **A coup** is a dump or rubbish tip. It can also be applied insultingly to an untidy place: 'His bedroom's a right coup.'

coupon   The face: 'Ye canny miss a coupon like that.'

crap   As well as the general meanings, the following constructions are common in less refined speech. To **crap it** or **crap your load** is to be afraid or to chicken out, and to **crap it off** someone or something is to be afraid of him or it: 'He craps it aff big Shuggie.'
　　As an adjective it means rotten, no use: 'This picture's crap.' A **crapper** or **crap-bag** is a coward.

crash   To lend or borrow, usually a cigarette: 'Crash us a fag, will ye?' 'Can I crash a fag off you?'

cuff   To inflict a heavy defeat on: 'A team a wee lassies could cuff that shower.'

curry-shop   A Pakistani or Indian restaurant.

cutter   To **run the cutter** is to act as a bookie's runner or simply to take another person's line to the betting-shop for him.

cut-up   When someone suspects corruption or dishonesty in a lottery, vote, or apportionment of rewards he may say 'It's a cut-up.'

Dead good at singing

da Familiar name for father: 'How's it gaun Da?' 'Where's yer da?'

dab To **let dab** is to let on, divulge something: 'She won fifty pound wi her premium bond an never let dab to her aul man.'

daftie A fool or a mentally-retarded person.

dale A high diving board or platform at the swimming baths: 'Ah dare ye tae dive aff the dale.'

damp, dampt Euphemisms for damn, damned: 'You're gauny break the damp thing ya haunless eejit.'

Dan A nickname for a Roman Catholic: 'Are you a Billy or a Dan?'

danger Chance or likelihood, used ironically when something expected or desirable is not forthcoming: 'Any danger of you gettin a round in?' 'D'ye think there's any danger of this bus comin the day?' **No danger** is an emphatic phrase meaning 'certainly, that is a certainty, etc.' 'Will ye be there the night?' 'Aye, no danger!'

daud *or* **dod** A piece or lump: 'He fell ower a big dod a wid.' 'Gie's another daud a yer malt loaf.'

19

dauner To **dauner** is to saunter or stroll: 'Here's wee Alec daunerin doon the road.' **A dauner** is a leisurely walk: 'I think I'll take a wee dauner through the park.'

day The **day** is a colloquial form of today: 'I've no been ower the door the day.' 'When are ye gaun?' 'The day.'

dead *or* **deid** Very: 'You're dead good at singin.' 'Deid gallus, isn't he?' The word is also used in pubs to describe drinks left unfinished on a table or the bar. Before clearing away a half-empty glass a barman or barmaid may ask: 'Is this pint dead?'

dearie mearie A local elaboration of dear me.

deck In common use to mean the ground or floor: 'Ah fun a poun note lyin on the deck at the bus-stoap.' 'She slipped in the canteen and her dinner hit the deck.'

desperate In urgent need of a visit to the toilet: 'Get a move on in there, I'm desperate.'

diddy A woman's breast or nipple. Also used as a mild insult meaning idiot. To **diddy around** *or* **about** is to act like a fool, mess about.

didgy [1] Another term for a dustbin.

didgy [2] Short for digital: 'Err's yer didgy watches, three fur a pound!'

dig up To annoy or deliberately provoke a clash with someone: 'He never startit it. The wee man was diggin him up.' If someone says 'Are you diggin me up?' this is roughly equivalent to 'Are you looking for trouble?'

dinger Pronounced to rhyme with ringer, to **go your dinger** means to be very angry, to fly into a rage: 'The aul man'll go his dinger when he finds out!'

dinner school Not an eating academy but a school canteen, the place where school meals are eaten: 'I'm back onto full time now the wean's goin to the dinner school.'

dizny Broad Glasgow pronunciation of doesn't: 'She dizny like coffee.' A standing joke about any place of work that is commonly regarded as inefficient is to call it "Disneyland" . . . a place where this dizny work, that dizny work, he dizny work, and so on.

20

dizzy To **give someone a dizzy** is to stand him or her up, deliberately not turn up for a date.

dog To **dog** school or **dog it** is to play truant. Someone who does this is called a **dogger** and may be required to carry a card to be signed by each teacher whose class he/she attends — a **dogger's card.**

doll No doubt a borrowing from American films, this is an affectionate term of address: 'Thanks for the lift, doll.' Your **old doll** is your mother.

doo A dove or pigeon: 'The doos in George Square urny feart a anythin.'

doobie A fool or idiot.

doocot *or* **dooket** A dovecote. Also used to mean a pigeonhole or a compartment in a desk: 'I was sure I put that letter in one of these dookets.'

doolander A heavy blow: 'He gave him a doolander on the nut.'

doolie A fool or idiot.

dot To go, especially quickly: 'I'll just dot down to the shops.' Also to wander: 'We spend Saturday afternoon dottin around the town.' Sometimes used mean pour or dash: 'Dot a wee drop more milk in my tea, will ye?'

dough-heid A name applied to anyone considered stupid.

Dough School Nickname for The Queen's College, formerly called the College of Domestic Science.

dout *or* **dowt** A cigarette-end. There's the old joke about the schoolboy who, when given a row by his father for smoking, says it's all right to smoke because Jesus smokes (the minister had told him to bring all his doubts to Jesus).

down In gambling circles a losing horse or bet is described as having **gone down**: 'The favourite in the three-thirty went down.' 'This line's down.'

dreep *or* **dreip** If you find yourself on top of a wall that you think is too high to jump down from one answer is to dreep it. This involves gradually letting yourself down by the hands, face to the wall, until you are at full stretch. You then let yourself drop the remaining height.: 'He was that bevvied he had to dreep the front step.'

drooth A great thirst: 'You've a right drooth on ye the night.' **Droothy** means very thirsty.

Drum, the   Nickname for the Drumchapel housing scheme: 'Ah'm gaun wi a fella that stays up in the Drum.'

dummy tit   A rubber teat for a baby, as enshrined in the devastating children's rhyme chanted at someone suspected of clyping:
>Tell-tale tit
>Yer mammy canny knit
>Yer daddy canny go to bed
>Without a dummy tit

dump   An apple-core or what's left after someone has finished with an apple: 'Starvin are ye? Want ma dump?'

dumps   A barbaric ritual observed among schoolchildren. On the day of a child's birthday anyone who finds out about it is entitled to give the lucky person a thump on the back for each year of his new age. This is called "giving him his dumps."

dunny   A cellar, especially at the bottom of the stairs in a tenement, a proverbially murky place: 'Ma daddy says there a big bogeyman doon the dunny.'

duster   To **go your duster** means to work very hard: 'Finished already? you've been goin your duster!'

dwam   A daze, a state of mental abstraction: 'It might help if you paid attention instead of sitting there in a dwam.'

dyke   Any kind of enclosing wall may be called a dyke: 'The wean's fell aff a dyke an hurtit his sel.'

Big Eat-the-breid

eat-the-breid   A nickname, usually applied to anyone having a big appetite: 'Big eat-the-breid's snaffled the last yumyum.'

eejit   A local pronunciation of idiot. **Eejit-heid** is a name applied to anyone considered stupid.

eekies   Equal, all square, or the same: 'You give me a pound and that's us eekies.' 'It's eekies to me whether I go or not.'

efter   Local version of after: 'Ah'll see yeez efter.'

El D   A familiar name for Eldorado, a proprietary brand of fortified wine. Also **L.D.**

electric soup   Vivid term for a mixture of meths and red biddy as drunk by alcoholic down-and-outs.

emdy   Local pronunciation of anybody: 'Emdy else comin up the road?'

err   Broad Glaswegian pronunciation of:
    1. there: 'Whit's at daein err?'
    2. air: 'That's that caper up in the err.'
    3. Ayr: 'Moan we'll go tae Err fur the day.'

evrubdy   Local pronunciation of everybody: 'There's nae need tae let evrubdy know yer business.'

F

Footering

faimly   A local pronunciation of family.

Fair, the   The annual Glasgow Fair occupies the last fortnight in July and is still the time when most Glasgow folk take their summer holidays. **Fair Friday**, the traditional last day of work before the holidays, is proverbially the greatest single bacchanal outside of Hogmanay. With many places of work closing down at lunch-time the fun is well under way by mid-afternoon. On the other hand **Fair Monday**, the following Monday, is one of the quietest days of the year. The city centre can look deserted as thousands are either away on holiday or recovering from the excesses of the weekend.

fairies   The dismissive description **away with the fairies** means daft, distracted, senile, in a dream: 'I can trust you with nothin; ye're away with the fairies half the time.'

faither   Local pronunciation of father. Often used as a term of address for any elderly man: 'Want a haun across the road faither?'

fankle   A tangle or mess: 'You've left all my papers in a fankle.' **fankled** means tangled up, in a mess: 'Och, my washin rope's all fankled.'

far enough   When someone dislikes or can't be bothered with something or someone he may say: 'I could see it (or him, etc.) far enough.'

feart   Frightened: 'Ah'm no feart fae you ya big bully.' A **feartie** is a coward.

filla   A local pronunciation of fellow: 'How's the wee filla?' Your **aul filla** is your father.

fine well   Perfectly well: 'I know fine well he got his jotters last week; he's just no lettin on.'

finger   Often pronounced to rhyme with singer.

Firhill   Home ground of Partick Thistle F.C. in the north side of the city, mecca for thousands of devoted followers whose attendance every other Saturday has been said to represent (to borrow a phrase from Johnson) "a triumph of hope over experience."

The ground's motto has become something of a catch-phrase: "Firhill for thrills."

five-eight   The phrase **just a common five-eight** is an expression used to describe an ordinary person with no airs or pretensions.

five-spot   Another obvious borrowing from the U.S.A., this means a five pound note: 'Emdy got change of a five-spot?'

fix out   To sort out, arrange, tidy: 'Give us a wee minute till I get my stuff fixed out.'

fleein   Another term for drunk, usually applied to the happy and lively stage rather than the morose or incapable: 'I realised the old boy was fleein when he started giein us "San Francisco." '

flier   A headlong fall: 'I'll murder you if ye leave that skateboard in the close again. I very near took a flier ower the damp thing!'

flit   To **flit** is to move house: 'When did ye flit from Castlemilk?' An instance of this is called a **flitting**: 'Here's a furniture van pullin up. There must be a flittin on.'

fly   Cunning, devious. **Fly for** means ready for, wise to the tricks of, experienced in: 'He tried to pochle it but we were fly for him.' 'It wizny your fault. Ye just wereny fly for it.'

flyman   A rather disapproving term for someone considered fly, that is cunning, devious, not to be trusted: 'Ah wouldny trust that wee flyman as far as Ah could boot him.'

footer To **footer** with or **footer about** with something is to fiddle or tinker with it, to mess about: 'Stop footering about with that screwdriver and give us a hand with this.'

Something described as **footery** is small, fiddly, or insignificant: 'These ha'pennies are footery wee things.' A **footery job** is one involving a great deal of fiddling about with small or awkward bits and pieces.

for When a person describes himself or someone else as being "for" something it means he is desirous of it or willing to do it: 'I'm for a pie supper.' Thus "what are you for?" is not an invitation to a metaphysical discussion on the purpose of life but means 'what would you like?'

fore To the fore means alive, in good health, around: 'Is your old grandad still to the fore?'

fu The Scots form of full, used as another word for drunk: 'Don't give him any more to drink, he's fu already.' This suggests an amusing image of a drinker as a kind of container with a finite capacity beyond which the contents are likely to spill.

fun A local version of found: 'Where did you get that video recorder?' 'Ah fun it mister, honest!'

Ginger

gadgie   An idiot or fool.

gallus   A fairly comprehensive term covering a range of values, such as cocky, sharp, bold, tough, flash, nonchalant: 'The wee man's got his gallus new jaikit on.' 'She comes wanderin in dead gallus like she owns the place.' 'He battered the pair a them — talk about gallus!'

   The word originally expressed disapproval, probably deriving from the idea of being fit for or likely to end up on the gallows, but is now firmly established as a term of praise.

game   Allowing for the variations in Glaswegian pronunciation this word can be pronounced as in standard English or to rhyme with 'hem'. Where a word is exclusively pronounced in the second way I have spelt it accordingly.

   That's the game is a general phrase of encouragement or approval. In the negative, **that's no the game**, it means 'that isn't right' or 'that isn't done.'

   Out the game A phrase borrowed from football where it usually applies to a player forced to leave the field by injury. In everyday speech it can mean exhausted, unconscious, or extremely drunk: 'Ah'm away for a wee lie doon — Ah'm just aboot oot the gemme.'

G

27

The game *or* **gemme** is a football match: 'Were ye at the gemme the day?' **Gemmy** is similar to the English 'game' in the sense of being plucky, and like gallus it can also mean sharp or flash: 'Ye should have heard him givin up cheek tae the bouncers, he's that gemmy!' 'Who's the big yin wi the gemmy waistcoat on?'

A **gemme kid** is a young person who is bold, cheeky, sharp, cool, or any permutation of these.

gantry The area behind a bar where spirit bottles are displayed or mounted on optics. The term is also applied to the range of spirits, especially malt whiskies, available in a particular pub: 'The wee Vicky Bar's got a crackin gantry.'

gaun A local pronunciation of go on. Used on its own or with an insulting name it is a term of rude dismissal: 'Gaun ya daft eejit ye!' **Gaun yersel** is a phrase of encouragement or approval, perhaps coming from football in the sense of a player making a lone run. I was once present at a rally in Queen's Park which was addressed by Tony Benn. Amidst the applause and cheering that followed his speech a wee Glasgow wifie was heard to cry: 'Gaun yersel Mr Bogeyman!'

Gaun is also a local pronunciation of going: 'Ah'm no gaun.' 'Was that you Ah saw gaun inty the Co?'

gauny Going to: 'Ah'm gauny loss the heid in a minute!' This also forms questions or requests (literally, are you going to) and is roughly equivalent to 'will you please': 'Gauny gie's a break, eh?' 'Gauny see if the rain's aff yet?' The negative form of this is **gauny no** (roughly, will you please refrain from): 'Gauny no swear in front a the weans ya bampot?'

geggie Sometimes shortened to **gegg**, this word for mouth appears only in contexts in which someone is advised to keep his closed: 'Just you shut yer geggie, pal.' 'Keep yer gegg shut.'

gemme, gemmy Dealt with under **game**.

gen up A question meaning 'is that true?': 'Ah've landed a job.' 'Gen up, have ye?'

Gers, the Nickname for Glasgow Rangers F.C.

28

get This is often used on its own meaning to go or be allowed to go: 'What like was the party?' 'Ach, I didny get.' Used as a command it means go away: 'Gaun, beat it, just get, will ye?'

Another meaning is to accompany or escort: 'Hang on a wee minute and I'll get you down the road.'

gettin Becoming. Interesting because it can appear at the end of a statement: 'She's awfy cheeky gettin' ie 'She's becoming very cheeky.'

ginger A general term for all varieties of fizzy soft drinks: 'Gie's a boatle a ginger, missis,' 'What kinna ginger, son?' 'Lemonade.'

give **Give someone into trouble** or **a row** is a local variation of get someone into trouble, land someone in bother.

glabber Sticky mud: 'Try an keep the dug oot a that glabber.'

glaikit Foolish, daft, stupid-looking: 'I feel glaikit with this daft hat on.'

glaur Thick greasy mud, mire.

Glesga, Glesca The *only* genuine broad Glaswegian pronunciations of Glasgow. Spurious alternatives like "Glasgie" spring from other parts of the country or the music hall.

go As a verb this has several different meanings:
  1. to be able to drive or handle: 'Can you go a bike?'
  2. to fancy or be ready for: 'I could fair go a wee cuppa.'
  3. to be able to understand or speak: 'It's a shame ye canny go the Gaelic.'

As a noun it is used to mean a fight, especially in the phrase **a square go** meaning a fair fight, unarmed, one against one. 'Do you want your go?' means 'Are you looking for a fight?'

gommy A **gommy** is a stupid person, a fool. **Gommy** can mean stupid or stupid-looking and **gommy-looking** means stupid-looking.

good To **take a good drink** means to drink fairly heavily on a regular basis. **Good style** is an adverbial phrase meaning well or briskly or in a pleasing or admirable manner: 'The boys are knockin back the pints good style.' 'The band was goin it good style.'

go through To go through someone means to give him a severe telling-off: 'If Mary had heard him talking lik that she'd a went through him.'

29

gowpin *or* **goupin**   Very sore, throbbing with pain: 'Gie's a seat, ma feet are gowpin.' 'My head's gowpin with that racket up the stair.'

granda, granpaw   Grandfather.

granma, granmaw   Grandmother.

greet   **To greet** is to weep, cry. **A greet** is a bout of crying. Someone who perpetually looks miserable or displeased may be described as **greetin-faced**. When two children have a dispute that ends in tears for one or both of them this is called a **greetin-match**: 'If you pair don't stop your argy-bargy there'll be a greetin-match in a minute.'

grey (or blue) van   The legendary vehicle in which the insane are said to be taken away to be locked up: 'The big grey van'll be comin for him any day now.'

grip   Someone who is behaving in a silly or overexcited manner may be requested to **catch a grip** or **come to grips**.

grog   **To grog** is to spit. **A grog** is a lump of spittle: 'Which wan a you ratbags grogged oan ma jaikit?'

grun   A local pronunciation of ground: 'There's a fiver lyin on the grun.'

gub   The mouth: 'Shut yer gub you!' **To gub** someone is to hit him in the mouth or defeat him soundly: 'I see the Gers got gubbed again.'

guddle   A tangle or mess: 'Don't leave the room in such a guddle this time.'

guttered   A popular term for drunk. Perhaps this implies such a degree of inebriation that the sufferer is compelled to lie in or make his way home via the gutters.

gutties   Sandshoes, plimsolls, baseball boots, etc.: 'Where's yer boots? Ye're no gettin a game in just yer gutties.'

guy   Guy meaning man or boy is in much greater use in Glasgow than elsewhere in Britain. Perhaps this is an indication of the deep influence of American films, particularly on the generation that grew up in the 30s and 40s: 'Lee'm alane, he's only a wee guy.'

That's Her Comin'

H

hackit   Ugly, unattractive, most often applied to girls: 'Chic got aff wi the big blonde and Ah wis left wi her wee hackit mate.'

haddy   A shortened form of haddock, used as a mild term of abuse; an idiot.

hail *or* **hale**   Whole: 'Ah'm scunnered wi the hale lot a yeez.'

hairy   A contemptuous term for a sluttish girl: 'What are ye runnin about wi that wee hairy for?'

half *or* **hauf**   A drink of spirits, especially whisky: 'Who's for a wee half?' A **half and a half-pint** is a time-honoured combination of drinks: a whisky with a half-pint of beer for a chaser. This is not so common amongst the younger generations who have developed a taste for more exotic concoctions.

halfers *or* **haufers**   To **go halfers** *or* **haufers** is to split the cost of something with another person: 'Me'n the wee brother's gaun haufers on a motor.'

hallelujah   The Salvation Army is sometimes referred to as the **Hallelujahs**: 'The Hallelujahs were at the door collectin.'
    To **go hallelujah** is to join the Salvation Army.

hammer To **give something the hammer** is to stop it or switch it off: 'Give that telly the hammer, will ye?'

Hampden (Park) The southside home ground of Queen's Park F.C. and Scotland's national stadium. At internationals the noise made by the assembled celebrants at times of excitement has long been famed as the **Hampden Roar**.

handers *or* **hauners** During a fight that is going against him (whether because he is outnumbered or outmatched by one opponent) someone may call for his friends to assist him. This is called 'shouting for handers' and may simply be a cry of 'Handers!' Also used as a verb: 'Is naebdy gauny hander us?' A **hander** is someone who fights by your side, or simply a friend or associate.

handless *or* **haunless** Clumsy, inept, butterfingered.

hang To **hang one on** someone is to punch him, usually in the face.

hanks Broad Glaswegian form of thanks: 'Ye're a wee gem, hanks a lot!'

Happy Larry Ironic nickname for someone considered to be miserable or a wet blanket: 'What's up wi Happy Larry the day?'

hardcase *or* **hardman** A man with a reputation for being tough or a good fighter.

haw An expression used to attract someone's attention: 'Haw mister, got the right time?'

head *or* **heid** To **put** or **stick the head on** someone is to butt him. A person who is becoming over-excited may be asked to **keep the heid**.

headbanger *or* **heidbanger** Sometimes shortened to **header**, this is a popular term for someone considered crazy, especially if dangerous. I assume it derives from the idea of a violent lunatic banging his head on a wall. This usage predates the contemporary alternative meaning of a heavy-metal enthusiast.

headcase *or* **heidcase** A lunatic.

heart-roasted A graphic term meaning annoyed, exasperated, at the end of your tether: 'They weans've got me heart-roastit wi their carry-on.'

heave To **give something the heave** is to throw it out or pack it in. To **give someone the heave** is to throw him out, fire him, or in the case of a lover to throw him over.

heavy   Standard draught beer. In England draught bitter comes as near as it can to this. A **wee heavy** is a small bottle of strong ale, usually containing just under half a pint.

heavy dunt, the   To **give something the heavy dunt** is to stop doing it or get rid of it. The phrase can alsooo be applied to a girlfriend or boyfriend: 'Is it no time ye were giein that wee toerag the heavy dunt?'

heavy team, the   Originally meaning a tough gang or the hardest members of a gang, this is now often humorously applied to any group of people who are supposedly to be feared.

heedrum hodrum   This is a disrespectful term applied by ignorant lowlanders to Gaelic song and bagpipe music: 'There's another of them Gaelic programmes on. I canny be annoyed wi aw that heedrum hodrum.'

hee-haw   Pronounced with accent on 'haw', this is not the call of a donkey but a coy substitute for a much stronger phrase meaning none or nothing at all: 'Ah put in thirty year at that place, an whit dae Ah get at the end of it? Hee-haw!'

heid-the-baw   A nickname, sometimes affectionate, sometimes meaning an idiot: 'Here he is, wee heid-the-baw himsel!' 'This place is full a bloomin heid-the-baws!'

heidie   Nickname for a headmaster: 'Watch it, the heidie's comin.'
    As a verb it means to head the ball: 'The winger slung ower a brilliant cross an the big man heidied it in.'
    Heidies *or* **headers** is a street football game played (either as singles or doubles) in a manner not unlike tennis. Goals are established fairly close together and play is started by one player throwing up the ball and heading it towards the opposite goal. It is possible to score directly in this way or the opposing player may be forced to save by catching the ball. Alternatively, the receiving player may head or volley the ball straight back, chest it down and kick it back, or allow it to bounce before kicking it back. If a goal is scored or the ball goes out of play the game restarts as above.
    Wee heidies is a version of this played in a confined space such as a close or shed.

hems   To **put the hems on** someone is to restrain him or prevent him from doing something: 'He used to like his bevvy but when he got married the wife soon put the hems on him.' The phrase is also used when something is ruled out or made impossible: 'There's the snow on again. I doubt that's put the hems on the game the morra.'

hen A term of affection for a girl or woman. It is often used when speaking in a friendly way to a stranger: 'Is that your glove you've dropped, hen?'

Her, Him The Anonymous Spouse. Many married people tend to speak of their beloved without referring to her or him by name. It is almost as if the marriage partner has attained such a talismanic status that it would be bad luck to utter the name aloud: 'I'll need to be away hame to give Him his tea.' 'I'm takin Her an the weans to the pictures the night.'

het In the children's game of Tig the player who is doing the chasing is said to be **het**: 'Tig! You're het!'

hielan The lowlander's version of Highland. In a similar way to the non-Irish use of the term Irish, hielan is also used to mean unsophisticated or daft: 'That's an awful hielan way of doing it.' A **hielanman** is a Highlander.

Hielanman's Umbrella Nickname for the area of Argyle Street beneath the great railway bridge leading to Central Station. The name arose from the place's use as a rendezvous for exiles from the Highlands and Islands: 'Ah got it in a wee shop in the Hielanman's Umbrella.'

high heid yin Usually ironic term applied to any person possessing relatively great power or authority.

hing[1] A local version of hang: 'Hing aboot, here a bus comin noo.'

hing[2] Broad Glaswegian version of thing: 'Ah'm gauny get wanny they hings, whit d'ye cry thum?' The final g is often dropped in compound words like **anyhin, everyhin, nuhin, sumhin**.

hingie Also called a **hing** or **hing-oot**, this is a time-honoured pastime for tenement dwellers:
1. Open a window facing onto the street.
2. Place elbows on window sill (if contemplating a long stint a cushion is recommended).
3. Hang out so as to be able to observe all that passes in the street or conduct a conversation with someone on the ground.

You are now having a **hingie**.

hingmy *or* **hingwy** Broad Glaswegian version of thingmy, what-do-you-call-it, or whatsisname.

hingy Slightly unwell, out of sorts: 'What's up wi ye? Ye're lookin kinna hingy this weather.'

34

hink   Broad Glaswegian version of think: 'Ah hink you're smashin, so Ah dae.'

hoachin *or* **hotchin**   Full of, infested with: 'The toon's hoachin wi wine baurs noo.'

hoachy   Lucky, "jammy", as in 'a hoachy goal'.

homer   A term applied to an official at a football match who appears to be biased in favour of the home side: 'We wis robbed — the ref wis a homer!'

honey   An attractive woman: 'Have ye seen his sister? A big honey!'

honk   Vomit, both verb and noun: 'Watch oot, this bam's gauny honk in a minute.' 'As if it wisny bad enough bein sick you have tae get honk aw ower yersel.'

honkin   Stinking or very bad: 'That picture was honkin.'

hooch   The exuberant 'spontaneous' cry of a Highland dancer: 'Yon accordionist never cracks his face. He just gives a wee hooch now and then.'

hooley   Originally Irish, this means a wild party: 'Are ye comin roon tae big Paddy's? There'll be a hooley on the night.'

horse in *or* **get horsed in**   To eat or drink heartily: 'Look at Tam gettin horsed in to his chicken korma.'

hot-pea special   A snack, sold in old-fashioned cafes, consisting of hot marrowfat peas dressed in vinegar.

how   The widespread use of this to mean 'why' causes great confusion to those unused to it and vice-versa: 'How did you come here?' 'Cause you telt me tae!' 'Sorry?'
   How no, of course, means why not.

howff   An old Scots word meaning a shelter or any meeting-place for cronies. It is still used in this sense to mean a labourers' shelter or hut on a building site or in a shipyard, etc.

how's it gaun   A conventional greeting, how are you? how are you doing?

howk   To dig. A miner howks coal, a potato-picker howks tatties, and logically enough a nose-picker howks his nose.

huckle   To throw someone out of or bundle someone into a place: 'When he startit shoutin an swearin the bouncers huckled him out.' 'Ah seen your Johnny gettin huckled inty a polis caur.'

hudgie   When an adventurous child takes a free ride by hanging onto the back of a moving lorry this is called **catching** or **taking a hudgie**: 'Away an catch a hudgie on a jumbo jet!'

hughie *or* **huey**   In full, **hughie bush**, this mean vomit. You might call it an inspired example of onomatopoeia: 'Efter Ah had a good hughie Ah wis right back inty the bevvy.' 'Watch yer feet, sumdy's hueyed on the steps.'

hullo!   Any piece of good fortune or eagerly-awaited event may be greeted with this exultant cry: 'There's yer tea out.' 'Hullo!'

humph   As a verb this means to carry, especially when a heavy load or long distance is involved: 'See taxis! Ah've had tae humph they cases aw the way fae the station.'
 As a noun it means a hump in the back: 'Ah'm gettin a humph carryin that pram up the stair.' To say that something **came up your humph** means that it occurred to you for no particular reason: 'What did ye do that for?' 'Ach, it just came up ma humph.' Someone who is disgusted or disappointed may say: 'Would that no sicken yer humph?' **Humphy** or **humphy-backit** means hunch-backed.

Hun   A nickname for a Protestant. Also a vague nonsectarian insult much used in football chants like 'The referee's a hun' or 'Go home ya hun.'

hunner   A local version of a hundred.

hunt   To chase away or run out of town: 'I'm no huntin ye, but is it no time for yer bus?' 'He's a rogue that yin — he should be huntit.'

hurl   A run, ride, or lift: 'Wait an I'll give ye a hurl down the road.'

hurtit   A past tense of hurt: 'He says it never hurtit him.'

hut   A past tense of hit: 'Who hut ye, son?' 'The dug got hut wi a lorry.'

His brain's away for ile

Ibrox Park Home ground of Glasgow Rangers F.C. in the south-west of the city.

icey *or* **icie** An ice-cream van: 'Away an get a bottle a ginger aff the icey.'

ile A Scots pronunciation of oil. The phrase **away for ile** means wasted, useless, finished, etc.: 'His brain's away for ile.'

into *or* **inty** This occurs in various contexts. **Get inty them** is a football supporter's advice to his team, urging them to set about the opposition with more vigour. Similarly **inty his heid** is a more specific way of saying 'get stuck into him' and **I'm inty your heid** means 'I'm going to set about you.'

   To **be into** something is to want it or some of it: 'No wantin yer puddin? I'm inty it, well.'

J

Got a light, Jimmy?

jag An injection: 'I never got gas at the dentist — he gave me a jag.' As a verb it means to prick or stick into: 'Somethin's jaggin me.' **Jaggy** means prickly or sharp: 'Mind the jaggy nettles.'

Jags, the Nickname for Partick Thistle F.C.

jaikit *or* **jaiskit** A local version of jacket.

janny Familiar term for a school janitor.

jaup A little drop or splash: 'Whoever painted that wall left wee jaups on the carpet.'

jaur A jar.

jawbox A sink, especially one of the old-fashioned boxed-in sinks with cupboard space underneath and, often, a window above it.

jeely Jelly or jam: 'Gie's a jeely piece, Maw.'
A **jeelly nose** is a bloody nose.

jeely-jaur A jamjar: 'Any auld jeely-jaurs? We're gaun fur tadpoles.'

jeez-oh A mild exclamation: 'The Jags are through to the final! Jeez-oh!'

jiggin, the   A dance: 'Are ye goin tae the jiggin the night?'

jile   A local pronunciation of jail. Used as a threat of vague but terrible punishment: 'You'll get the jile if they dishes urny done when Ah get hame.'

Jimmy *or* **Jim**   Well known as a convenient term of address for a male stranger: 'Got a light, Jimmy?' It seems to have all but replaced older forms like 'Jock' or 'Mac'. Of course this kind of thing is not exclusive to Glasgow; we all know from television that in London it is the done thing to address every male as 'John'.

jine   A local pronunciation of join. A **jiner** is a joiner.

jing-bang   The lot, everything: 'Ah'm sick an tired of the whole jing-bang.' Sometimes used as an adjective: 'Ye mean tae say he lost the whole jing-bang lot?'

jink   To dodge or weave about. The former Celtic player Jimmy Johnstone was nicknamed 'Wee Jinky' for his elusive dribbling.

joco   Nonchalant, unperturbed: 'He never battit an eye — just walked away whistlin, quite joco.'

jorries   Marbles. Someone with a posh accent is often said to talk with **a jorrie in his mouth**.

jotters   The same as cards, in the sense of a worker's employment documents held by his employer. Thus to **get your jotters** means to get the sack.

jook *or* **jouk**   To dodge or duck: 'Ah just jooked under the wire.' To **jook aboot with** means the same as **jump about with**.

juke   The phrase **up your juke** means up the front of your clothing: 'The rain was comin on so I shoved the papers up my juke.'

jump   To **jump about with** is to associate with, hang around with: 'He jumps about wi big Archie an his mates.' To **jump in** means to get involved in an ongoing fight: 'What a rammy! Evrubdy wis jumpin in!' **Jumpin** means very angry: 'By the time Ah got hame the wife wis jumpin.'

Jungle, the   Nickname for the 'Celtic end' at Parkhead.

just *or* **jist**   Tacked on to the end of phrases to indicate briefness or moderation: 'Can ye no wait five minutes just?' 'Ah'm only wantin wan or two jist.'

K

His patter's magic — we were aw knottin' oursels

keech   Pronounced with ch as in 'loch', this means muck, especially excrement: 'Ma shoe's aw keech.' Sometimes used as a term for a despicable person.

    Keechy means mucky, covered in something disgusting.

keek   To peek: 'Somebody's keekin through the curtains.' Also a noun: 'Have a wee keek out an see if emdy's comin.'

keekabo   Local equivalent of peekaboo.

keeker   A black eye: 'Who gave ye the keeker then?'

keelie   A familiar term for a Glaswegian. Depending on the person using it this can be either affectionate or insulting. Jack House dedicates his book *The Heart of Glasgow* to ''the salt of the earth — the Glasgow keelie'' but to many people the word denotes a hooligan or vulgar lower-class person.

keepie-uppie   Footballing game of juggling with the ball using feet, knees, head — anything other than hands. One of the legends attached to the Scotland-England football fixture is that during Scotland's 1967 Wembley victory Scotland's dominance over the then World Cup holders was so complete that Jim Baxter was able to play keepie-uppie with the ball.

Kelvinside accent 'Posh' accent typical of the residential West End, by means of which 'sacks' come out as 'sex', etc. There is nothing more ludicrous than someone who affects this imperfectly.

keys In children's games if someone gives a double thumbs-up and says 'keys' this gives him immunity from whatever consequences the game involves: 'Tough! Ye never had yer keys up.'

kick To **kick with the left foot** means to be a Roman Catholic.
To **kick with the wrong foot** means to profess a religion regarded as unsuitable: 'Nae chance of gettin a game for them. Ye kick wi the wrang fit.'

kicking A severe beating: 'You're on a kickin, pal.'

kilt A past tense of kill: 'Big Gerry hauf-kilt him.'

kin A local pronunciation of can: 'She kin speak French nae bother.' This also appears in various compound forms like **kinnah** (can I), **kint Ah** (can't I), and **kint Ah no** (can I not): 'Kinnah get wan a yer sweeties?' 'Ah kin aye come back the morra, kint Ah?' 'Kint Ah no? We'll see aboot that!'

kinna Kind of: 'Look out an see what kinna day it is.' 'Ah feel kinna funny.'

knacked Exhausted, broken, useless: 'Ah'm knacked!' 'Try this yin; that yin's knacked.'

knock To steal: 'Wee Angela's got liftit for knockin stuff oot a Woolies.' A **knocker** is a thief.

knock back To refuse or reject: 'They got the offer of a house in Darnley but they knocked it back.' A **knockback** is a refusal or rejection: 'How is it every time Ah ask a bird for a dance Ah get a knockback?'

knot To **knot yourself** is to laugh uproariously, be in stitches: 'His patter's magic; we were aw knottin snsels.'

L

Where did ye get him – in a lucky bag?

laldy   To **give someone laldy** is to give him a thrashing or beating. To **give it laldy** is to do something vigorously or enthusiastically: 'The band's been givin it laldy aw night.'

lamp   This can mean to strike ('He lamped him wan') or to throw ('Lamp that oot the windy').

Lanny   Nickname for Lanliq, a proprietary brand of cheap fortified wine.

lavvy   Short for lavatory: 'Aye that's him; the wan wi the hair like a lavvy-brush.'

lavvy-diver   A disparaging term for a plumber.

lay   To **lay it off** to someone is to tell him about something in an insistent and lengthy manner: 'Ma heid's nippin wi her faither layin it aff tae us aboot the S.N.P.'

leader-aff   The leader of a gang.

lee   A local form of leave, as in 'Lee us alane' 'Lee me some', etc.

left-footer   A slang term for a Roman Catholic.

lend   Often pronounced len, this is a local form of loan: 'Gauny gie's a len a yer drill.' To **take a lend** or **loan** of someone is to take advantage of him, especially in a way that makes him look stupid: 'They've got you for a mug, pal; they're takin a right len a ye.'

length   **The length of** means as far as: 'Are you goin the length of Pollok?'

line   1. A betting slip or the copy of it held by the punter; also the bet itself: 'I've put four wee lines on.' 'She's got a line up.' 'That's a winnin line.'
   2. A special discount arrangement to be used in a designated shop or warehouse: 'A woman in the work's got a line for Goldbergs.'
   3. A **doctor's line** or **sick line** is a medical certificate issued by a G.P. to certify that someone is unfit for work.

Lisbon Lions   Nickname for the Celtic team that won the European Cup in Lisbon in 1967, the first British side to win the trophy.

Lodge, the   The Orange Lodge.

long enough   A long time: 'If ye miss yer bus ye've tae wait long enough for the next wan.'

look   To **get your head looked** is a popular phrase for having a psychiatric examination. This usually crops up in contexts where someone recommends such an examination for an acquaintance: 'He needs his heid looked if he buys that motor.'

loss   A local form of lose: 'Pit that in yer bag an ye'll no loss it.' This is logical enough when you consider that the past tense is 'Lost' (loss-ed?).

loupin   Very sore: 'Ma big toe's loupin.' Also infested or crawling: 'That wean's mockit — Ah bet ye he's loupin an aw.' 'The West End's loupin wi artists.'

lucky bag   A novelty for children, sold in sweet shops, consisting of a sealed paper bag containing sweets and an unknown small toy or trinket, usually cheap and tawdry. Its proverbial place in the dialect is shown by such ironic usages as 'Where did ye get him — in a lucky bag?'

lumber   **A lumber** is a member of the opposite sex that you 'get off with' at a dance, party, etc.: 'We were at the jiggin last night; couldny get a lumber, but.'
   To lumber someone is to 'get off with' him or her: 'Ma pal got lumbered by your big brother.'

M

A *Midgie Raker*

ma A local version of my: 'Ah've lent ma video tae ma mammy.'

ma, mammy, maw Various versions of mother.

maddy A **maddy** is a lunatic. To **take a maddy** is to lose your temper in a big way.

mad skull A reckless, possibly dangerous person: 'Here comes that mad skull next door on his motorbike.'

malky A **malky** is a safety razor used as a weapon. **To malky** someone is to cut him with a razor. To **get malkied in** is to set about someone or something with a will. My understanding of the term's origin is that it was originally rhyming slang: Malky (short for Malcolm) Fraser = razor. Who Malcolm Frazer was (or is) is not clear.

man Husband: 'She's fell oot wi her man.'

manky Dirty, grubby, in need of a wash: 'That boy aye comes hame manky.' It can also mean dirty in the sense of obscene: 'Ah've read that — it's pure manky.'

mark Used as a verb meaning to scar: 'Ah'll mark ye.'

44

masel   Myself.

mask   Of tea, to infuse: 'We'll just give the tea a wee minute to mask.'

melt   To **get into someone's melt** is to attack him, beat him up. This seems to derive from the Scots use of melt to mean spleen and is therefore an admirably precise and graphic phrase, anatomically speaking. **To melt** someone is to hit him a hard blow: 'Beat it or Ah'll melt ye wan.' Jamieson's *Dictionary of the Scottish Language* gives a charmingly full definition: "To knock down; properly, by a stroke in the side, where the *melt* lies."

mental   Insane: 'Stay away fae that yin — he's pure mental.' To **go mental** is to become so enraged that your sanity seems open to doubt. **A mental case** is an insane person.

merrit   A local version of married: 'Is she the wan that merrit ontae the McLeans?'

mess   To **mess** is to meddle or interfere, but is extended to mean to provoke or start a fight. Phrases such as 'don't mess' or 'nae messin' are intended as salutary warnings against provocative behaviour. **A messer** can be someone who makes a mess but also a troublemaker or belligerent person.

messages   Shopping: 'I'm away for the messages.' Messages are carried in a **message bag.**

messin   A small dog or puny person; now used mainly as a mildly insulting name, of the kind adults might use for a child: 'Get out of that bunker ye dirty wee messin!'

mibby   A local version of maybe: 'Ach, Ah'll mibby no bother goin.'

midden   A dustbin or rubbish tip. Also used as an insulting name for a dirty or despicable person: 'Are you gauny lie in yer scratcher aw day, ya dirty aul midden?'

midgie   A dustbin or, in tenements, the shelter in the back court where these are kept: 'Sling that aul thing in the midgie.' A **midgie-man** is a dustman and a bin-lorry is a **midgie-motor.** A **midgie-raker** is a tramp who combs through dustbins for things of value to him.

Milk *or* **Mulk, the**   Nickname for the Castlemilk area of the city: 'We've been six years in the Milk.'

mince   Mysteriously enough this prosaic word for humble fare has blossomed into one of the most versatile words in the dialect.

It is used to mean nonsense, rubbish: 'Yer heid's full a mince', 'He talks a lot a mince.' It is also a general term for anything unpleasant that finds its way to somewhere it shouldn't be: 'The back a ma jeans is aw mince!'

Extremes of denseness are also measured by it: 'He's as thick as mince.' Someone who is listless or lacking in animation may attract a comment like: 'What's up wi you? Ye're sittin there like a pun a mince.'

If a person succeeds in spoiling something for someone else, taking the wind out of someone's sails, etc., he might say: 'That's sickened his mince for him.'

mines   A local version of mine: 'Gie's at back, at's mines.'

ming   To **ming** is to stink; **a ming** is a bad smell. **Mingin** means stinking but can also be used to describe anything bad: 'We just came hame early cause the weather was mingin.'

miraculous   Usually, who knows why, pronounced 'marockyoolus', this is a slang term for drunk. 'Maroc' is sometimes heard as a shortened form of this and has nothing to do with tangerines: 'Ah seen him stotin roon Georgie Square, pur maroc he wis!'

miss   To **miss yourself** is to miss having a good time by not being present: 'Big Joe's party was rare; aye, ye missed yersel.''

mix   To **put the mix in** is to deliberately stir up trouble between others: 'Me'n him was always good mates till she startit puttin the mix in.'

moan   A local form of come on, shortened from c'moan: 'Moan you, get a move oan!'

mobbed   Crowded: 'The town was mobbed the day.'

mockit *or* **mawkit**   Extremely dirty: 'Ye're no walkin on ma good carpet wi they mockit boots on.' It can also mean rude, disgusting, obscene, etc.: 'See him, his mind's pure mockit.'

model lodging house   A hostel for the single homeless, often shortened to **model**: 'Ye can go an stay in the model for aw Ah care.' Someone who lives in a model is known as **a modeller.**

molocate   Used mainly by children, this means to batter or destroy: 'Ah'm gauny molocate you!'

46

moolly Mean, miserly, stingy: 'Ye'll get nothin oot a that moolly aul devil.'

mooth Mouth: 'He's a mooth on him like the Clyde Tunnel.'

moothie Mouth-organ: 'Get the moothie oot an gie's a wee tune.'

morra, the Tomorrow, or to be more precise the morrow: 'See yeez the morra then.'

multi A familiar term for a multi-storey or high-rise tower block: 'It's murder stayin in a multi when the lifts urny workin.'

N

A No-user

naebdy *or* **nobdy**   Local versions of nobody: 'Who's is that's, naebdy's?'

naw   Local version of no: 'Mair snaw? Aw naw!'

neb   As a noun this can mean:
1. the nose: 'Some neb on him, eh?'
2. A nosey person: 'That aul neb wants tae know aw yer business.'
3. An instance of prying or being nosey: 'You just want them to ask us in so's you can have a good neb round the place.'

To neb is to be nosey, to pry.

neck   To **go on your neck** is to have a nasty fall, especially by slipping and falling over backwards: 'The ice on that pavement's diabolical — that's twice Ah've went on ma neck.'

To ask for a bottle of beer **by the neck** means that you want to pour it yourself or use the glass you already have: 'Pint a heavy an two big Newkies by the neck.'

ned   A criminal or hooligan: 'Partick police are on the look-out for two neds who walked out of a local hostelry carrying the Space Invaders machine.'

neebur   Neighbour, often used as a friendly term of address: 'How's it gaun, neebur?' Even more friendly is the shortened form **neebs**: 'Want a run up the road, neebs?'

nick   To go quickly, dash: 'I'm just nickin out for a pint of milk.' To **nick about** can mean: 1. to wander around a place, to be seen around and about: 'I often bump into him nickin about the South Side.' 2. To move around a lot, be very active, especially in socialising: 'Your wee brother nicks aboot a bit disn't he?' 3. To associate with: 'How long have ye been nickin aboot wi that mob?'

night, the   Tonight: 'Naw, it's no the night, it's the morra night.'

nineteen-canteen   A very remote time in the past: 'Is it no time she was retirin? She's been here since nineteen-canteen.'

nip   To hurt, be sore, as in 'Ma heid's nippin.' On the other hand, to **nip someone's heid** is to nag him or give him a row: 'Ma maw's always nippin ma heid aboot sumhin.'
   To **nip a wee burd** is one way of saying pick up a girl.

nippy sweetie   A jocular term for a drink of spirits: 'How about a nippy sweetie to finish off?' Also used to describe a bad-tempered person: 'Just keep out of that yin's road; she's a bit of a nippy sweetie.' The derivation is from the sense of nippy meaning sharp-tasting, burning to the taste, etc.

no   Not: 'Ah'm no gauny tell you again.'

nock   Clock: 'Is that nock right?'

noo *or* **now, the**   Now, at this moment: 'Are ye goin the now?' Perhaps through the influence of 'just now' you will often hear an 's' creeping into this, giving versions like **s'now, isnow, the snow**: 'Is that it startin isnow?'

no-user   A shiftless or useless person: 'How did she go an marry a big no-user like him?'

nuhin   Broad Glaswegian form of nothing: 'Whit are you sayin?' 'Nuhin.'

nut   A form of no, usually confined to one-word answers: 'Is that yours?' 'Nut.'

nyaff A lovely expressive word for a (usually small) annoying or contemptible person: 'Get aff ya nyaff!' In his *Dictionary of Slang* Eric Partridge suggests the word may have something to do with the Parisian slang *gniaffe,* an abusive term for any man. This conjures up an amusing image of an auld alliance of Glaswegian and Parisian keelies. It may be that there is a distant relationship here but I'm inclined to think that the current use of the word comes from the following Scots terms as delightfully defined in Jamieson's *Dictionary of the Scottish Language:*

> **nyaff** V. n. 1. to yelp; to bark, 2. Applied to the pert chat of a saucy child, or of any diminutive person.
> **nyaffet** a diminutive, conceited chatterer.

Ooyah

oary boat   A rowing boat: 'Ma Daddy took us tae Queen's Park for a shot in an oary boat.'

odds   To **shout the odds** is to harangue or shout long and loud at someone: 'There's that loony next door shoutin the odds at his mother again.'

offie   Short for off-licence: 'Moan we'll nick doon the offie for a few tins.'

old   **Old boy, old man, old fella, old yin** all mean father: 'Tell yer aul boy Ah wis askin for him.' The equivalents for mother are **old dear, old doll, old girl, old yin**: 'Ah'm away for the messages for the aul dear.'

Old Firm   Nickname for Rangers and Celtic considered together as an institution in Scottish football: 'It's another Old Firm final.'

ony *or* **olny**   Local variants of only: 'Ah'm ony ten.'

oose   Dust, fluff: 'How'm Ah gauny get aw this oose aff ma good velvet jaikit?' **Oosey** means dusty, covered in fluff.

ooyah   An exclamation of pain: 'Ooyah! Get aff ma fit!'

outsider   The thick crusty end slice of a loaf of bread: 'Who wants an outsider?'

51

P

Patter Merchant

pa *or* **paw** Father.

Paddy's Market Famous *al fresco* market in and around the Briggait selling mainly second-hand (at least) clothes and old furniture. The vendors' stock is conveniently arranged on old tables or areas of pavement and its somewhat haphazard appearance has secured for this market a proverbial place in the dialect: 'Away an tidy up your room—it's gettin like Paddy's Market in there.'

pamp To sound a car horn; also the noise this makes: 'That'll be the taxi pampin noo.' 'Gie the horn a wee pamp.'

pan To **knock your pan in** is to exhaust yourself by working very hard: 'Ah've been knockin ma pan in up that ladder aw day.'

panel **On the panel** means absent from work, having been certified unfit by a doctor. This phrase is a survivor from the former 'panel' of non-paying patients treated by certain GPs.

pan loaf   An oblong loaf of bread with a fairly soft crust all round it, as opposed to a plain loaf which usually has a harder, darker crust but only on top and bottom.

A **pan-loaf accent** is a posh accent. There are two possible explanations for this usage known to me: the first being that a pan loaf was considered the kind of bread that posh people ate, the second being that pan loaf is rhyming slang for toff as pronounced locally.

pap   To throw: 'Just pap that in the bin.' To **pap out** is to throw out or reject: 'He got papped oot the techy college.'

pape   A fairly rude name for a Roman Catholic, obviously a contraction of papist.

Paradise   Name given by the faithful to Parkhead, home ground of Celtic FC.

paralytic   Falling-down drunk. This is often heard pronounced paralettic.

parish   **On the parish** is a rather old-fashioned way of saying on the dole. To **join the parish** means to sign on.

Parkhead   Home ground of Celtic F.C., also known as Celtic Park.

parkie   Short for park-keeper: 'The parkie'll check ye if he sees ye ridin yer bike on the grass.'

patter   A person's line in conversation. This can mean ordinary chatting, as in 'Sit doon an gie's aw yer patter'; it can also mean talk intended to amuse or impress, as in 'He's got some patter that pal a yours', or any kind of insider's language, as in 'Ye'll get naewhere if ye don't know the patter.'

To **patter away** is to chat in an easy friendly manner. A **patter-merchant** is a usually derogatory term for a glib or would-be persuasive talker or for someone who thinks he is a comedian.

pawnies *or* **ponnies**   Short for pontoon: 'Who's for a wee game a pawnies then?'

peely-wally   Pale, ill-looking: 'Are ye awright? Ye're awfy peely-wally the day.'

peep   To **put someone's gas at** (or sometimes **in**) **a peep** is to crush him in an argument, take the wind out of his sails, or shut him up: 'Ah soon telt her. Ah soon put her gas at a peep.' This seems to derive from the old gas lighting mantles that could be turned down to a very low flame (a peep).

peever The game of hopscotch, or more particularly the stone or crushed tin can used in this.

people **We are the people!** is a cry or chant often heard from football supporters in the bizarre belief that the often arbitrary or temporary success of their team confers on them some kind of elite status as human beings.

pep Peppermint cordial, as in 'A dark rum an pep, please.'

petted lip The sign of a spoilt or sulky child, that is, the lower lip protruding in front of the upper lip: 'Never mind the petted lip. You're not going and that's that.'

photie Short for photograph, but sometimes applied to any picture: 'She's awful holy; she's got the hoose full a saints' photies.'

piece A sandwich or slice of bread with something spread on it: 'He takes pieces to his work.' 'What's on your piece?' Pieces are carried in a **piecebox** or **piecetin.**

place To **lose the place** is to lose your temper or your head.

plank As a verb this means to hide (something), stash it away: 'Plank the carry-out behind the settee.' As a noun it means a hiding place or secret cache: 'The old boy's got a half-bottle in a wee plank somewhere in the house.'

play To **play yourself** is to amuse yourself, mess about or waste time: 'Here Ah'm knockin ma pan in an youse are just playin yersels.'

playpiece A snack given to a schoolchild for consumption at playtime. Despite the name this isn't necessarily a sandwich: 'What have ye got for yer playpiece?' 'A Mars bar.'

plootered Drunk.

pluke *or* **plook** A spot or pimple, sometimes a term for a despised person: 'What's that wee pluke wantin?' It can be used as a verb meaning to squeeze (a pimple): 'Ye better plook that before it gets any bigger.' **Plooky** means spotty: 'Naw, no the wan wi the plooky face.'

plump A sudden downpour of rain: 'Get the washin in, there's gauny be a plump.'

plunk To **plunk school** is to play truant. **A plunker** is a truant. Both these terms are now rather old-fashioned.

pochle   **To pochle** something is to obtain it or win it by cheating, fixing, or fiddling: 'McGinley won the raffle.' 'Pochled it ye mean.' **A pochle** is a swindle, a fixed competition, or fiddle.

poke   A bag, especially a paper bag: 'Put your crisp-poke in the bin now.'

pokey-hat   An ice-cream cone: 'Run down to the ice-cream van and get an oyster and two pokey-hats with raspberry.'

polis   The police or a policeman: 'Her man's a polis.' **Murder polis!** is a general exclamation of shock or fear.

problem   Phrases like 'What's your problem?' or 'You got a problem?' are not, as may first appear, indications of a desire to give assistance but fairly aggressive challenges or indications that violence may follow.

prod *or* **proddy**   A Protestant. This derives from the common pronunciation of the full word as Prodestant. **Proddy** can also be an adjective.

puggled   Although it can mean just plain daft, this usually means drunk to the 'silly' stage, i.e. clumsy, forgetful, giggly, etc.: 'You must've been puggled when you put that shelf up.'

puggy   This is a Scots word for monkey, but the relevance of this to the various uses given here is not always obvious. **Fu as a puggy** means very drunk or full (having overeaten). You can also be **fat as a puggy**. To **take a puggy** is to lose your temper or 'do your nut' as in 'The boss'll take a puggy if he sees this.' In card games the kitty is sometimes called **the puggy**: 'Right, who's no chipped in tae the puggy?'
    The word is also used to mean a one-armed bandit or fruit machine, and I have also heard of it being used for an automatic cash-dispenser outside a bank: 'Ah just pit ma kerd in your puggy an it swallied it!'

pump   To **pump** is to fart. A **pump** is an example of this.

pun   A local variation of pound (weight): 'Three pun a totties please.'

punt-up *or* **puntie-up**   A means of helping someone to climb onto or over something. Putting your back to the wall, etc. you interlace the fingers of both hands to form a kind of stirrup into which another person can put his foot. He can then put his other foot on your shoulder and scramble up.

punter In Glasgow this does not only mean a gambler. It can mean simply any person at all: 'A gallus wee punter.' It can also carry overtones of low standing on the social scale: 'Anything'll do for the punters.' 'He's just a punter like the rest of us.'

pure An adjective or adverb meaning absolute, absolutely, expressing the height or depth of whatever it is applied to: 'She's pure rotten tae me.' 'It was a pure shame, so it was.' 'That dinner was pure magic.' 'That yin's a pure ratbag.'

A queerie

queer   A **queer difference** means a substantial difference: 'There's a queer difference between walking it and getting a lift.'

queerie   Unlike most parts of Britain in Glasgow this does not mean a homosexual but merely an odd or eccentric person.

quoted   **Well-quoted** means highly-regarded, well-esteemed: 'I hear the challenger's well-quoted.' **Not quoted** means given no chance, unimportant or useless: 'Never mind what that balloon thinks—he's no quoted.'

R

Ah'll rattle your ear fur ye

ra   Really broad Glaswegian for the: 'Me'n ra boays're gaun tae ra gemme.'

rag   To **lose the rag** is to lose your temper.

rammy   A brawl or a bustling crowd: 'Ah'm just back from the sales—what a rammy!'

randan   **On the randan** means on a spree of debauchery, especially heavy drinking: 'No feelin sae good this mornin? On the randan last night, eh?'

rare   Usually pronounced rerr, this is used to mean excellent, highly enjoyable: 'That was a rerr picture!'

rattle   To hit someone a sharp blow, usually on a specified part of the body: 'I'll rattle yer ear for ye'.

red raw *or* **rid raw**   Used in describing parts of the body that are red and sore, for such reasons as working in water or exposure to cold: 'Ma hauns are rid raw wi washin they sterrs.' 'Aw the wee soul's nose is red raw wi the cold.'

refreshment   The most popular euphemism for an alcoholic drink is **a wee refreshment:** 'It's not unknown for Big George to take a wee refreshment of a Saturday night.'

riddy A red faced caused by embarrassment. Also something that is a source of embarrassment: 'There Ah'm staunin no knowin the fly's open—what a riddy!'

rift To rift is to belch. A rift is an example of this.

right The phrase **that'll be right** or **that will be right** is an ironic or sometimes angry riposte meaning exactly the opposite, i.e. there's no chance of that, you certainly will not, etc.: 'He said what? Aye, that'll be right!' This phrase has its own equivalent in rhyming slang: 'That'll be shining bright.'

rip To rip someone is to slash him with a knife or razor: 'Get lost or Ah'll rip ye.'

room and kitchen A small tenement flat consisting of a bathroom and two rooms, one of which contains cooking facilities. Some people choose to sleep in the kitchen bed-recess, keeping the other room as a sitting room. Others use the kitchen as a sitting room and the other room as the bedroom.

Rossy Local pronunciation of Rothesay, a traditional holiday resort for Glaswegians.

Rottenrow, the The Glasgow Royal Maternity Hospital in Rottenrow: 'Ma sister's in the Rottenrow the noo.'

row Pronounced to rhyme with how, this means to wind, as in 'Row up the nock', i.e. wind up the clock.

rummle To jostle, disturb, upset: 'That big centre-forward should get in amongst the defence and rummle them up a bit.'

run-out To **do a run-out** is to eat a meal in a restaurant and then abscond without paying; a most unsavoury practice.

S

Sannies

sad Used mainly by schoolchildren to describe anything they regard as unjust or undesirable: 'Mair homework? That's pure sad!' Someone whom they consider to be mentally unstable may be labelled **a sad case** or **saddie** for short: 'Don't mess wi him, his big brother's a right saddie.'

sangwidge A local version of sandwich: 'Don't say "pieces", Justin, it's "sangwidges".'

sannies Short for either sandshoes or sandwiches.

sapple To rinse or wash out. As a noun it can mean an instance of this: 'I'll just give the teapot a wee sapple,' or a soapy lather.

Sarry Heid Nickname for the Saracen's Head in the East End, Glasgow's oldest pub (the present building is not the original) known, shall we say, for being somewhat rough and ready.

scaffer A tramp or low-life person: 'Where did ye dig up that aul coat? Ye're gaun aboot like a scaffer.'

scheme   Not a cunning plot but the local term for a new housing estate such as Darnley or Drumchapel, usually associated with remoteness from anywhere and few amenities: 'There no wan decent shoap on the hail scheme.' Come to think of it, perhaps there is something Machiavellian about the planning of these places.

scratcher   One's bed: 'Ach, Ah'll away tae ma scratcher.'

screw   **Screw the bobbin** or **screw the nut** are phrases roughly equivalent to 'get a grip of yourself, calm down, see sense, etc.' 'Screw the bobbin will ye! Ah canny get tae sleep wi that blimmin cassette gaun.' 'The gaffer says Ah've tae screw the nut or Ah'm gaun doon the road.'

screwtap   A beer-bottle with a screw-off top. Immortalised by the late Matt McGinn in his pastiche of *Raindrops are falling on my head* which came out as *Screwtaps are fallin on ma heid.*

scud   This means a slap or glancing blow, or to give such a blow: 'Ah'll scud your lug in a minute.' **In the scud** or **in the scuddy** means naked, in the nude. Shock value is heightened by inserting the word 'bare' as in 'They were lyin on the beach in the bare scud!'

see[1]   Used in constructing sentences that refer the listener to someone or something that is the subject of the statement to follow: 'See this weather? Would it no sicken ye?' This is sometimes taken to ludicrously involved lengths: 'See me, see ma man, see chips? We hate them.'
     See if is a way of saying 'what if' or simply 'if': 'See if Ah'm gaun tae Shettleston, what bus dae Ah get?' 'See if you're no back in five minutes, you're for it.'

see[2]   To pass or give to someone else: 'See me ower that spanner, will ye?' 'Da says ye've tae see me a shot on yer bike.' 'See's a wee kiss, hen.'

sel   A local version of self: 'Hear aboot the lonely prisoner? He wis in his sel (cell).'

selt   A past tense of sell: 'Have ye no selt yer hoose yit?'

session   A **session** or **bevvy-session** is a spell of drinking, a booze-up. Sometimes shortened to **sesh**: 'That was a rare wee sesh last Friday.'

shape   An oddly-shaped person: 'Nice-lookin, him? He's a wee shape!'

Shawfield   Home ground of Clyde F.C. Also used as a race-track for greyhounds: 'Is Chic's dug runnin at Shawfield the night?'

shed   A parting in the hair: 'Is my shed straight?'

sherbet dab   A confection for children consisting of a paper bag containing a small lollipop and some sherbet. The idea is to lick the lollipop and dip it into the sherbet.

shilling   **Not the full shilling** and **threepence off the shilling** are used to describe someone considered stupid, 'not all there.'

shilpit   Applied to a thin, undernourished, or weak-looking person: 'She's no goin wi that shilpit object is she?'

shin   A plural of shoe: 'Wait till I get my shin on.''

shirrackin   A severe telling-off: 'The aul dear gave us a shirrackin for losin ma Transcard.'

shoodery   When an adult lifts a child up to sit on his shoulders (shooders) to carry him or allow him a better view in a crowd this is called giving him a shoodery: 'Ah could see nuthin till ma dad gied us a shoodery.'

Shoo, Shooey, Shug, Shuggy   These are all nicknames for anyone called Hugh: 'Big Shuggy's lookin fur you.'

shoot   To **shoot the crow** means to depart, leave, make yourself scarce: 'By the time I got there the boys had shot the crow.'
   A possible explanation for this is that it could be rhyming slang: shoot the crow = go.

shows   A general term for any kind of funfair or carnival: 'If you're good your Granny'll take you to the shows tomorrow.'

shuge   A local version of huge: 'Mammy, there a shuge big motor stoapt ootside.'

shy   In football, a throw-in: 'It's our shy.'

sick   **On the sick** means off work through ill-health.
   A **sickener** is a crushing blow, a reverse bad enough to make you sick: 'That was a right sickener he got when they told him he wasn't gettin a company car.'
   Sickened you! is the triumphant cry of a person who has proved someone else wrong: 'Daddy says it's no yours it's mines so sickened you!'

sideyways   A local version of sideways: 'Me, bevvied? Naw, Ah always walk sideyways.'

sin An injustice, a crime: 'It's a sin what he's to put up wi wi her, so it is.'

single In a chip-shop anything bought without chips is described as single, as in **a single fish, a single pie.**

single end A one-room flat in a tenement building.

sink In football, a fan wishing one of his side to put in an effective tackle on an opposing player may cry: 'Sink him!' or 'Sink the boot on him!'

sinker A dirty look or withering glance: 'He drew me such a sinker I wisht I'd kept my mouth shut.'

siver The gutter running beside a pavement: 'Ah fun a ten-bob bit in the siver.'

skate it To win a contest easily: 'It'll no be much of a match, that. The boys should skate it.'

skelf A splinter of wood that gets stuck in a finger. Also applied to a very skinny or small person: 'The weight's fell aff her—she's nuthin but a skelf.'

skelly Cross-eyed or squinting: 'He's got me skelly watchin they damp videos aw night.'

skip To avoid paying for your ticket on public transport is to skip your fare: 'Thinks he's gemmy cause he skipt his fair on the subway.'

skite This can mean a glancing blow, as in 'a skite round the ear' or to strike with such a blow, as in 'hailstones were skitin aff his cagoule.' It can also mean to slip or slide: 'Watch, that pavement's dead slippy—evrubdy's skitin aw ower the place.' **On the skite** means on a spree, a prolonged drinking bout: 'Ye look like ye've been on the skite fur a week.'

skittery This can be a contemptuous way of describing something small or insignificant: 'There's only a skittery wee drop left.' It is also used to suggest that something is likely to upset the stomach: 'Naw, Ah never take a pint a that—it's kinna skittery stuff, is it no?'

skoosh A general term for any fizzy soft drink: 'Gie's a slug a yer skoosh.' It is also used to mean anything easily accomplished: 'The drivin test wis a skoosh.' An alternative form of this is **skoosh-case:** 'Four nuthin tae the boys—a pure skoosh-case!'

To **skoosh it** means to do something easily or win by a mile.

sky   In football this is used as a verb meaning to kick the ball high into the air, usually unintentionally: 'There he wis, open goal, an the big diddy skies it ower the baur.'

slag   **To slag** someone or something is to make insulting or disparaging remarks about him or it: 'His mates are aw slaggin him for gettin a Mohican.' **A slag** is an insulting comment.

I have it on good authority that schoolchildren nowadays give each other insulting nicknames known as **slag-names**: 'Ma right name's Archie an ma slag-name's Cokynut-heid.'

sluch   To drink or eat soup noisily: 'Ye're pittin me aff ma tea wi yer sluchin.'

slug   Another borrowing from the U.S.A., this means a drink from a bottle: 'Want a slug a ginger?'

slunge   To rinse, wash out: 'Gie's a wee drap watter till Ah slunge ma mooth.'

smash   Coins, change, as opposed to paper money: 'I've got a pocket full of smash.'

snottery   Although this derives from snotters, Scots for snot, this word is often used in a wider sense to mean in any way displeasing or contemptible: 'Away ye go ye snottery aul devil!' 'There's only a snottery wee drop left.'

snyster   A quick snack or bite; a titbit: 'Ah'm no really hungry. Ah just feel like a wee snyster.'

sook   **A sook** is someone who sucks up to his superiors, a toady. To **sook in** is to suck up to someone: 'Never mind tryin to sook in wi me.'

Sooside   The part of Glasgow lying south of the Clyde. Someone who lives here is a **Soosider.**

sore hand   Jocular term for a big jammy piece (jam sandwich) which makes the eater's hand look as if it is wrapped in a blood stained bandage.

sore wan   A general term for any painful injury: 'Ah tripped ower the stair carpet this mornin; got a right sore wan tae.'

soul   Often pronounced to rhyme with foul, this is a term expressing pity or affection: 'He's got nobody to come home to, the soul.' 'That's a good wee soul, makin yer aul mammy a wee cuppa tea.'

spare   A collective noun for unattached women: 'Is there gauny be any spare at this party?'

special   Many brands of heavy beer call themselves Special. This is often shortened to **spesh**: 'What is it, special?' 'Naw, gie's a lager, Ah'm aff the spesh.'

specky   Nickname applied to anyone wearing glasses; also used as an adjective: 'Who's the big specky wan?'

speug *or* **speuggie**   A sparrow: 'Ah always pit some breid oot fur the wee speuggies in the wintertime.'

Spiders, the   Nickname for Queen's Park F.C. whose home ground is Hampden Park.

square go   Dealt with under **go.**

square sausage   Also called Lorne sausage, this seemingly cubist delicacy is simply sausage meat cut into rough squares: 'See England? See if ye ask fur squerr sausage, they look at ye as if ye were daft.'

squinty   Local variant of squint: 'Ah still say ye've pit that picter up squinty.'

stairhead   In a tenement close the landing at the top of each flight of stairs is called the stairhead. In the bad old days this was where shared toilets might be located: 'Ah've opened the sterrheid windy tae let some err aboot the place.'

stank   The metal cover or grille over a drain in the street: 'He's drapt his key doon that stank.'

start   A new employee is often referred to as a **new start**: 'Tell the new start big Rab says he's tae go for a long stand.'

stay   To live, dwell, have one's abode: 'Ah've steyed in this close fur twenty-nine year, son.' 'Where does your pal stay?'

steamboats   A picturesque if somewhat inexplicable word for drunk: 'Look at the state of him—steamboats again!'

steamed   To **get steamed in** to something or someone is to set about it or him with a will: 'Never mind waitin till Ah get mine; just you get steamed in, son.' 'He beltit doon the sterr an got steamed right inty him.'

steamie A communal wash-house. There are few, if any, of these left but their reputation for being hotbeds of gossip lives on. The phrase **the talk of the steamie** describes something or someone that is (or deserves to be) the subject of gossip or scandal: 'Is that another fella ye've got? You'll be the talk of the steamie ma girl.'

steamin Another word for drunk.

stiffen To knock out or beat up: 'Just you try it an Ah'll stiffen ye.'

stir To **stir it** is to deliberately cause trouble between others: 'We've enough bother wi'out you comin round stirrin it.' Someone given to this kind of behaviour is known as a **stirrer.**

stoat To bounce: 'Hey you! Chuck stoatin yer baw aff this windy, right?' Heavy rain is often said to be stoatin down. To **stoat about** means to bustle or simply to move around: 'Ah've been stoatin aboot the toon aw efternin.' In football, when play is restarted by the referee bouncing the ball between two opposing players this is called a **stoat-up.**

stoater This can mean a particularly good example of anything but its most common use is in relation to attractive women: 'Have ye seen that burd Bill's gaun wi noo? A wee stoater!'

stooky Plaster, probably derived from stucco. A **stooky** is a plaster-cast on a broken limb, or a stupid or excessively formal person. **To stooky** someone is to hit him very hard, knock him out. This has obvious similarities to stiffen.

stooshie A row, uproar, or brawl: 'There'll be a right stooshie when this gets out.'

stormer Anything excellent: 'That yer new guitar? It's a stormer.'

stotious Yet another word for drunk.

stowed *or* **stowed out** Pronounced to rhyme with loud, this means packed, absolutely filled with people: 'The Quaich was stowed last night.'

stramash A word beloved of football commentators, meaning a confused tussle: 'It must be! No, off the line! Driven in again by . . . what a stramash in the goalmouth!'

stumer A fool or idiot.

66

sub crawl   A Glasgow variation on the pub crawl. The idea is to get off at every subway station and have a drink in the nearest pub. N.B. there are fifteen stations on the Glasgow underground.

subs   Boots. In football, to **put the sub on** someone is to kick him.

Subway   Glaswegian name for the Underground.

Sufferin General   Nickname for the Southern General Hospital.

sugarollie   Licorice. **Sugarollie-water** is an old-fashioned home-made soft drink made by shaking pieces of licorice in a bottle of water. The term is still applied by drinkers to beverages considered too sweet or weak: 'Ah'll stick tae the Guinness — yon stuff's like sugarollie-water.'

sumdy   Local version of somebody: 'Sumdy gauny answer that phone?'

supper   In a chip-shop a combination of anything with chips is called a supper, even at midday. Fish and chips is **a fish supper,** pizza and chips **a pizza supper,** and so on.

sure   Used in a statement when the speaker is seeking confirmation: 'Sure we're on holiday on Monday?' 'It's no ma turn, sure it's no?'

swally   Pronounced to rhyme with rally, this is a local version of swallow: 'She's swallied the hail lot!' **A swally** can be a drink or a drinking session: 'Fancy a wee swally?'

swatch   Pronounced to rhyme with catch, this means a look at something: 'Give us a swatch at your paper.'

sweary word   A somewhat precious term for a piece of foul language: 'The only time he looks at a dictionary is to look up sweary words.'

sweetie-wife   A talkative or gossipy person: 'Would ye listen tae him — he's like an aul sweetie-wife.' Presumably, lady confectioners were well-known for being chatty.

T

A right hard ticket

tail   Usually used in relation to money, **on your tail** means in your possession, to your name: 'Ah arrived at Euston wi naewherr tae stay an a fiver oan ma tail.'

tackety boots   Hobnailed boots: 'See them up the stair? Ye'd think they went aboot wi tackety boots on.'

take   To be afflicted by, as in take a bad back, take a bad turn, take a heart attack, and so on.

By analogy, I suppose, with to take in washing, someone paid to clean other people's stairs in a tenement is said to **take in stairs.**

If someone says 'I'll take my hand off your jaw' this does not mean that unbeknownst to you he is resting his hand on your jaw but that he intends to strike you on it.

Tally   Italian: 'Ye canny whack the real Tally ice-cream.'

tank   To beat soundly: 'Scotland'll tank that shower.' It can also mean to travel at high speed: 'This time tomorrow we'll be tanking up the M.1.' A **tanking** is a sound beating, a heavy defeat.

taur   A local pronunciation of tar.

tea   The phrase **your tea's out** literally means your evening meal is on the table, but it is also used to mean you're for it, you've had it now. To call someone a **teaboy** is to imply that he is a toady.

team   A gang: 'He said he'd be back the night wi a team ahint him.' Used in several gang titles like the Govan Team.

tear   Pronounced terr, this means a jaunt or spree: 'That wis a rerr terr we hud in Millport.'

Teddy Bears   Nickname for Rangers F.C. The fact that this is rhyming slang becomes clear when you know that Bears is pronounced Berrs and thus rhymes with Gers.

teem   Heavy rain is said to teem down: 'It's been teemin aw day.' Also used as a noun to mean a downpour: 'We just made it back before a big teem came on.'

telt   A past tense of tell: 'That wean'll need tae learn tae dae whit he's telt.'

ten-bob bit   A fifty-pence piece: 'The machine takes ten-bob bits.'

teuchter   A Lowlander's term for a Highlander, not exactly insulting but not to be used to a Highlandman's face: 'The wee sister's gaun oot wi a teuchter.' 'Ah wis in wan a they teuchter pubs in Argyle Street the other night.'

that   Used to mean so or to such an extent: 'Ah'm that fed up Ah could spit!' **That's me, you, us, him, her, them** are expressions used when something is considered finished: 'OK that's you, off ye go.' 'She's only three days to go an that's her.' 'Just one more load an that'll be us.'

there   Often used to mean there is or there's, as in 'There nane left' 'There a man at the door' 'There wan there.'

they, thame   Local forms of those or them: 'Ah don't like they kinna fillums.' 'He's bought wan a they French motors.' 'Ah'll have wan a thame.' 'Ah'll go wi youse but nae way am Ah gaun wi thame.'

thingmy, thingmyjig, *or* **thingwy**   Term for a person or object whose name eludes the memory: 'Know who Ah met the day? Thingmy!' 'Ah've come away wi'oot yer thingwy.'

Thistle, the   Short for Partick Thistle F.C.: 'Ah thought her aul man wis a bluenose—turns oot he's a Thistle supporter.'

thon   That or yon: 'Ah'm away tae see thon filla at the bank.' 'Ah'll pit up wi a lot but Ah draw the line at thon.'

thought   In the phrase **it's a thought** this is used to mean something involving great effort or something approached with reluctance: 'Aye, it's a thought gettin up these dark mornins.' 'After a long break like that it's a thought goin back to your work.'

'Tic   Nickname for Celtic F.C.

ticket   A person, as in a **hard ticket** (a tough guy) or a **useless ticket** (a shiftless person, good-for-nothing).

tig   The local name for tag, the children's chasing game. The child who catches or manages to touch another will shout: 'Tig! You're het!'

tim   To empty: 'Tim yer cup an I'll gie ye some fresh.'

Tim   A nickname for a Roman Catholic: 'Heard the score fae Parkheid? The Tims'll be greetin the night.'

toe-ender   In football, a kick with the toe of the boot. Also used in other contexts: 'If I've to come down the stair to you you'll get a toe-ender.'

toley   Local term for the act or product of defecation. Sometimes used as a name for an objectionable person.

toon   A Glaswegian does not go into the city centre, he goes **up the toon**.

tore   To **get tore in** to something or someone is to set about it or him with vigour: 'She wis gettin tore inty him wi her handbag.'

torn-faced   Miserable-looking, wearing an aggrieved or hard-done-by expression: 'Ach, ye kin dae nuthin right fur that torn-faced aul crab.'

tother   This is an invented word. The expression **nae tother,** meaning no trouble, is a contraction of 'nae tother a baw' which is a kind of deliberate spoonerism of 'nae bother at aw.'

totty   A potato. For some reason **totty-peelin** means snobbish or posh when applied to an affected accent: 'An her wi that totty-peelin voice as if Ah didny mind wherr she wis dragged up.'

toty   Tiny or very young: 'Seen our new puppy? It's a toty wee thing.'

trainies   Training shoes: 'The bouncer knocked us back for havin trainies on.'

tube   A contemptuous term for a stupid or otherwise despicable person.

tummle   Tumble. The phrase **take a tummle to yersel** means liven up your ideas, get yourself sorted out, see the error of your ways, etc.

tumshie   A turnip. **Tumshie** or **tumshie-heid** are names for a stupid person.

turkey   To **stuff your turkey** is to eat heartily, cram yourself with food.

twicet   Twice: 'That's twicet Ah've telt ye — Ah'm no tellin ye again.'

two-up   A local term for the rude two-fingered V-sign: 'He started it. He gied us the two-up.'

Does this bus go to the Uni?

um   Broad Glaswegian pronunciation of him: 'Ah telt um no tae bother.'

Uni, the   Nickname for Glasgow University. Strathclyde University tends to be referred to simply as Strathclyde: 'Just think. Ma wee lassie gaun tae the Uni in the Autumn!'

urny   Local version of aren't, as in 'Youse urny gaun,' 'We urny comin,' 'They urny here.'

Me an' Joe'll verse you an' Rab

verse To oppose at football or some other contest: 'Me'n Joe'll verse you an Rab.' This is based on misconstruing versus (as in Clyde versus Queen's Park) as a verb 'verses'.

vicky A local term for a rude V-sign: 'We gied them the vicky an got aff wur mark.'

voddy Nickname for vodka: 'See's two heavies an two wee voddies.'

W

Doon The Watter

wabbit   Tired-out, lacking in energy: 'Ah'll no bother gaun. Ah'm a wee bit wabbit.'

wae   Broad Glaswegian pronunciation of with: 'We'll need tae leave it. We canny take it wae us.'

wallies   Pronounced to rhyme with rallies, this is a local term for false teeth: 'Ah canny whistle since Ah got ma new wallies.'

wally   (Rhymes with rally) When applied to an ornament this means made of china, as in **a wally dug** a china dog. **A wally close** is a tenement close that has tiling on the walls. Such closes are considered posher than those with painted walls.

wan   Local version of one: 'Whit wan's yours?'

wanner *or* **wanny**   Local version of 'oner' i.e. one go: 'He knocked his pint back in a wanner.' **To wanner** someone is to hit him a single hard blow: 'He widny shut up so Ah just wannered him.'

wanst   Once: 'Ah only went the wanst. It wis garbage.'

warmer   A term for someone who exasperates or disgusts you: 'They've been sittin daein nuthin aw day — whit a perr a warmers!'

waste To spoil or mar: 'Don't let the wean play with your book or she'll waste it.' To say 'I'll waste your face' is to threaten disfigurement to someone. Waste can also mean spoil in the sense of over-indulge: 'Their granny's got they weans wastit.'

    Wastit-face is a name applied to someone who looks petulant or spoiled. To say to someone 'Your heid's wastit' implies that you think he is stupid or 'away with the fairies'. On the other hand, to say 'My heid's wastit' is to confess you are too exhausted to think clearly.

watchie A watchman, as on a building site.

watter Water. To go **doon the watter** is a time-honoured expression meaning to go for a pleasure-cruise from Glasgow down the Clyde to such resorts as Gourock, Dunoon, Rothesay, and Millport.

wauchle To shuffle or waddle: 'Here aul Tony wauchlin doon the road.'

way The phrase **on your way** can be a rude expression of dismissal or a cry of encouragement: 'What're you doin hingin aboot here? On yer way pal!' 'That's your baw McNulty! Yes! On yer way wee man!'

wean (Pronounced wain) a baby or young child. Someone behaving childishly or showing fear about something trivial may be called a **big wean**: 'Gie the boys their baw back ya big wean.' 'Och it's only a wee jag, don't be such a big wean.'

weather **This weather** means these days, as in 'How're ye gettin on this weather?'

wee This is often used to mean young or younger, without reference to size: 'Ye never telt us yer wee brither wis bigger than ye.'

    A comparative form of wee exists in speech, but how do you spell it?: 'Naw, still too big. Have ye no got a wee-er wan?'

wee goldie An affectionate term for a glass of whisky: 'Ah'm fur a wee goldie this time.'

wee man A friendly title for a small person: 'Look who it is — how's it gaun wee man?' Someone wishing to register disgust, amazement, exasperation, etc. without resorting to profanity may say: 'Aw in the name a the wee man!' Perhaps this is a euphemism for the Devil.

wee team Used to designate a reserve team, irrespective of the size or age of the players.

well When this turns up at the end of a phrase it is roughly equivalent to then: 'Ye don't like liver? Don't eat it, well.'

well-fired Applied to bread or rolls, meaning baked to the extent that the crust or outside is almost black: 'I'll take six crispy rolls, well-fired ones if you've any.'

wellied Another word for drunk: 'Some folk can leave it at one or two jars — how do you always have to end up wellied?'

well on Yet another term for drunk: 'Course, the pair of us were well on by this time.'

well seen Obvious, to be expected: 'Is that you hame already? It's well seen your boss is on holiday.'

welly A local use for **welly** or **welly-boot** is to denote an ugly woman: 'Where'd ye dig up that welly-boot ye were oot wi last night?' To **give someone the welly** or **welly-boot** can mean to break off with a girlfriend or boyfriend or to sack an employee.

went A local equivalent of gone: 'If Ah hid knew Ah widny've went.' 'She's no here, she's went oot.' Also used in relation to doorbells, phones, etc.: 'Ah wizny in five minutes when the phone went.'

whack, cop yer Dealt with under **cop.**

what If in a pub you are asked 'What is it?' this is not a riddle or guessing game but an enquiry as to what you would like to drink: 'It's my shout. What is it boys?' 'What are you on?' is a similar question.

wheech Pronounced with ch as in 'loch', **to wheech** is to move (something) away very quickly: 'Who's wheeched the last empire biscuit?' 'Give us a list of yer messages an I'll wheech down to the shops.'

wheesht Wheesht! or **haud yer wheesht!** means be quiet!

wid¹ Local version of would. **Widny** is the negative: 'Ah widny take ye in a lucky bag.'

wid² Local version of wood: 'A big daud a wid.' **Widden** means wooden: 'There a man wi a widden leg.'

wife *or* **wifie** A woman, usually of mature years: 'Away an tell that aul wifie she's forgot her change.' Your **old wife** is your mother.

wilkies   To **tummle your wilkies** is to do a somersault. This derives from 'tumble like wildcats.'

willn't, willny   Local forms of will not or won't: 'Bob said he willny make it the night.'

winch   To **winch** can mean to go out with a member of the opposite sex: 'Yer mammy an me used tae go for walks in Rouken Glen when we were winchin.' If asked 'Are ye winchin?' this means do you have a steady girl-friend or boyfriend? To winch can also mean to kiss and cuddle: 'We spied them winchin in oor back close.'

windy *or* **windae**   Window. The phrase **out the windy** means ruled out, made impossible: 'He says his motor's knackered—that's the trip tae Loch Lomond oot the windy.' A somewhat different use is seen in **yer bum's out the windy** which is a graphic way of saying 'you are making an exhibition of yourself by talking nonsense.' While on the subject of spectacles, some people refer to their glasses as **windies**: 'Haud the paper a minute till Ah get ma windies on.'

wine-mopper   A down and out alcoholic who drinks cheap strong wine. Sometimes shortened to **mopper**: 'He couldny finish his pizza supper so he gied it tae an aul wine-mopper in George Square.'

wise   To say that someone is **not wise** is to imply that he is foolish: 'Hear what he was rushed for that suit? The boy's no wise.'

work   A factory: 'Here Howden's work comin oot noo.'

workie   A workman: 'That's terrible the mess they workies left on the pavement.'

wrang   Local version of wrong. Understanding this pronunciation is essential to the following joke.
   Customer in bakery: 'Is that a doughnut or a meringue?'
   Shop assistant: 'Naw ye're deid right missis, it's a doughnut.'

wrecked   Exhausted, tired-out: 'By the time I get home on a Friday night I'm too wrecked to go out.'

wulk   Local version of whelk. **Full as a wulk** is a nice, if inexplicable, term for drunk.

wulln't, wullny   Broader pronunciation of willn't and willny: 'Wullie wullny go.'

wummin   A local pronunciation of woman. It is quite commonplace to address an unknown lady as **Mrs Wummin**: 'Aw hey Mrs Wummin! Ye've drapt yer brolly.'

wur   a local version of our: 'What's fur wur tea the night?'

A yap

-y   In broad Glaswegian the word 'of' is often pronounced in such a way that it sounds like a 'y' tacked on to the end of the previous word: 'Wanny they hings', 'Somey thame's no use.'

ya bass   Belligerent phrase affixed to gang names in graffiti or slogans: 'Tongs ya bass!' Presumably this derives from 'you bastard' rather than from calling someone a fish.

yap   A gossip or talkative person: 'Ah've had tae listen tae that aul yap aw the way up the road!'

ye   A form of you ('Ye canny whack it') that can become plural ('Ah'll get yeez!'). Often added at the end of a phrase to increase the vehemence of name-calling: 'Away ye go ya mug ye!'

yes!   Cry of enthusiastic approval: 'Cop this pint. I managed to get served before the bell,' 'Aw yes big man!' 'What a baw! Shoot! . . . Yes!'

yin   A local form of one: 'That yin's mines.' It can be applied to a person ('She'll come to no good, that yin') and is often used in nicknames or terms of address, as in **big yin, wee yin, auld yin, young yin.** The fact that Billy Connolly is known as The Big Yin has occasioned some confusion down south and I remember hearing him introduced by an English TV announcer as the big *Yin*. No doubt millions assumed this was some kind of derogatory term for a Scotsman.

yon time   A popular expression conveying an unspecified but very late hour: 'What wi the buses bein aff Ah never got hame till yon time.'

yop   To **yop** in school slang means to tell tales, inform on someone. A **yop** or **yopper** is an informer, a clype.

yous   A plural form of you: 'Are yous comin an aw?'

y's   Gents' underpants: 'What a riddy! Tryin tae climb in the windy in ma y's!'

yuck it   A local variant of chuck it: 'Ah've had enough snash fae you so just yuck it, awright?'

yumyum   A kind of cake perhaps best described as like a doughnut without a hole, stretched to an oblong shape and sometimes containing jam: 'Away to the baker's an get four treacle scones, four snowballs, an four yumyums.'

Rhyming slang

A fair amount of rhyming slang is in everyday use in Glasgow. A great deal of this is, of course, not exclusive to this part of the world and I have attempted to include only such examples as seem to me to have a particularly Glaswegian flavour. This consideration has led me to leave out such popular usages as **china** (china plate = mate) on the grounds that this is as well-known in London as in Glasgow.

As with all pieces of rhyming slang that consist of two words it is always possible that only the first word may be used with the second part (that usually provides the rhyme) understood but not spoken.

corned beef Deef, i.e. deaf. Sometimes shortened to **corny.**
cream crackered Knackered.
cream puff The huff: 'Aw don't take the cream puff.'
Donald Duck Luck, esp. as in 'It's just yer donald.'
gone an dunnit Bunnit.
Gregory Pecks Specs, i.e. glasses. Sometimes shortened to **gregories.**
Hampden Roar Score, as in 'What's the Hampden Roar?' i.e. 'What's going on?'
hoosie Fraser House of Frazer, i.e. razor. Sometimes shortened to **hoosie.**
harry hoof Poof, i.e. male homosexual.
hi-diddler Fiddler, i.e. violin player.
hillbilly Chilly: 'Better take yer jaikit—it's turned a bit hillbilly.'
iron lung Bung, i.e. a tip.
Jungle Jim Tim, i.e. a Roman Catholic: 'Ah never knew he wis a Jungle Jim.'
kelly bow Dough, i.e. money.
mammy mine Wine.
Mars bar Scar.
Mick Jagger Lager: 'Three heavies an a Mick Jagger.'
Oscar Slater Later, as in 'See you Oscar Slater.' The man in question was involved in a famous Glasgow murder case.
pea pod This is unusual in that it is rhyming slang for another piece of rhyming slang, i.e. 'on your pea pod' = 'on your tod' = 'on your Tod Sloan' = 'on your own.' 'Emdy come roon last night?' 'Naw, Ah wis on ma pea pod aw night.'
pearl diver Fiver, i.e. a five-pound note.
pineapple Pronounced with the stress on 'apple' this means chapel: 'He's away tae the pineapple.'
radio rental Mental, i.e. crazy.

Rossy (Rothesay) Docks Socks.

St Louis Blues News.

satin and silk Milk.

scooby doo Clue, sometimes shortened to **scooby,** as in 'Ah haveny got a scooby.'

soapy bubble Trouble: 'You're gauny end up in soapy bubble, pal.'

wine grape Pape, i.e. a Roman Catholic.

winners and losers Troosers, i.e. trousers.

Phrases and Sayings

another clean shirt an that'll be me, you, him, etc. Ironical saying used when someone is slightly ill (with a heavy cold, for example); implies that the person is not long for this world: 'That's a terrible cough!' 'Aye, another clean shirt an that'll be me.'

as deep and dirty as the Clyde Applied to a devious, cunning, or untrust-worthy person.

as high as a kite Very excited, full of high spirits: 'The weans're always as high as kites the day before the holidays.'

as slow as a wee lassie Dilatory, lackadaisical.

as sure as guns (is iron) Certainly, without a doubt: 'He'll have forgotten his keys again, sure as guns.'

away an . . . Several phrases of rude dismissal begin in this way. Here are a few relatively inoffensive ones: 'away an bile yer heid, away an bile yer can, away an raffle yer doughnut, away an run, away an claw yer semmit.'

aw the nice! Exclamation of delight with schmaltzy overtones: 'Is this your Sadie's wean? Aw the nice!'

bite someone's ear To speak to someone nicely in order to get something out of him: 'When the joiner's finished bite his ear for a daud a wood.'

bother your shirt (*or* **arse** *or* **backside**) Usually found in the negative, this means to stir yourself, make an effort, give a damn: 'Ah telt ye tae go afore it got busy but naw, ye never bothered yer shirt.'

can't see green cheese Applied to a person showing envy or signs of wanting something just because someone else has it: 'Naebody thought aboot a tracksuit till Ah got wan—yeez canny see green cheese.'

couldny run a menage Applied to a careless or inefficient person. The local pronunciation is menodge: 'Imagine that big stumer a manager—he couldny run a menage.'

82

cruisin for a bruisin Applied to a person seeming to court danger: 'Ya cheeky peasant! You're cruisin for a bruisin.'

daft as a ha'penny watch Implies that sense is not to be expected from the person so described.

don't give us your worries Stop moaning: 'Just get on wi it an don't gie's yer worries, right?'

do you think I came up the Clyde on a bike? Do you think I'm daft? Alternative forms of river transport include a banana boat and a wheelbarrow.

do you think my head buttons up the back? Do you take me for a fool?

hair like straw hangin oot a midden Applied to dirty or unkempt hair: 'Ye're no gaun oot like that? Yer hair's like straw hangin oot a midden.'

he gets his shoes made at John Brown's His feet are so big that his shoes have to be constructed in a shipyard.

hell mend you More or less equivalent to 'I wash my hands of you'. This is addressed to a person who despite all warnings continues in a course likely to bring trouble on his own head.

his (or her) face is tripping him (or her). He or she looks very unhappy.

hunger and a burst Used to describe a state of scarcity or inaction followed by a glut or sudden feverish activity: 'Ah've been on tae the Clenny for weeks aboot shiftin that aul mattress an that's them came twice the day. It's always a hunger or a burst wi that crowd.'

I could eat a scabby dug (dog) I am extremely (not to mention indiscriminately) hungry.

if at first you don't succeed, in wi the boot an then the heid Robust local variation of the proverb.

if Ah don't see ye through the week Ah'll see ye through the windy Somewhat feeble parting witticism.

I'm meltin away to a greasy spot I am suffering from the heat or from overwork.

like a fart in a trance Rather rude way of describing a dreamy person or someone at a loss for something to do: 'Away oot fur gooness sake insteada hingin aboot the hoose lik a fart in a trance!'

like Sauchiehall Street Very crowded, busy, noisy, etc.: 'I came in for a quiet seat an it's like Sauchiehall Street in here.'

like snow off a dyke Disappearing very quickly, melting away: 'All Ah says wis "Emdy gauny len us a fiver?" and they aw vanished lik snaw aff a dyke.'

mammy daddy! Mock exclamation of fear or alarm.

a mouth like the Clyde Tunnel Applied to a loudmouthed or talkative person.

never died a winter yet A would-be cheery parting shot at the end of a discussion of the miseries of winter or of any disaster.

price of fish An unofficial index of the cost of living, brought in to add weight to a complaint: 'What wi that an the price a fish Ah'm fed up!'

sufferin duck! Exclamation of exasperation, annoyance, surprise, etc. Obviously a euphemism, but why a duck?

the baw's up on the slates Said when a plan falls through or something happens to put a stop to some activity: 'Wee Billy canny make it an he's the only wan wi a motor an aw. That's the baw up on the slates noo.' The phrase springs from street football: if the ball ends up on a high roof the game is effectively over.

the nights are fair drawin in Literally this means it is starting to get dark early these days, but this is rarely used seriously. It is more often used as a humorous remark to break an awkward silence.

to a band playing Used to describe great enjoyment of an activity, as in 'I could eat sausages to a band playing.'

up to high doh Over-excited or full of nervous tension: 'Thank Goad ye're back! The aul wife's up tae high doh.'

waste of space Applied to someone or something regarded as worthless: 'He's a no-user that yin — a pure waste a space.'

whit is it wi you? Addressed to a person who is persistently annoying: 'Gauny shut up a minute? What is it wi you, anyway?'

why are we so good? Football fans' chant when their team is doing well in a game, as if amazed at the arbitrary good fortune lavished on them by the gods.

wouldny say eechie or ochie The phrase means he wouldn't say yes or no, wouldn't commit himself. Jamieson's *Dictionary of the Scottish Language* records a variation 'I can hear neither eeghie nor oghie' and derives eeghie from 'igh or eighi' which means 'not' in "Sueo-Gothic, ancient language of Sweden." So there you are.

you'll get your head in your hands (to play with) You will be severely punished: 'If your homework's not done by tomorrow you'll get your head in your hands.'

your arse in parsley A rude, if poetic, way of saying 'you're talking nonsense'.

your face in a tinny A less rude way of saying 'Nonsense!' Sometimes shortened to 'Yer face!' A tinny seems to be a tin jug, but I confess ignorance as to why one's face should be in it.

your heid's full a broken bottles, penny whistles, mince Your head is full of nonsense.